# CHINATOWN

# CHINATOWN

AN ILLUSTRATED HISTORY OF THE CHINESE COMMUNITIES OF VICTORIA, VANCOUVER, CALGARY, WINNIPEG, TORONTO, OTTAWA, MONTREAL, AND HALIFAX

PAUL YEE

JAMES LORIMER & COMPANY LTD., PUBLISHERS
TORONTO

James Lorimer & Company Ltd. acknowledges the support of the Ontario Arts Council. We acknowledge the support of the Government of Canada through the Book Publishing Industry Development Program (BPIDP) for our publishing activities. We acknowledge the support of the Canada Council for the Arts for our publishing program. We acknowledge the support of the Government of Ontario through the Ontario Media Development Corporation's Ontario Book Initiative.

The Canada Council | Le Conseil des Arts
for the Arts | du Canada

40 YEARS + 40 ANS

ONTARIO ARTS COUNCIL
CONSEIL DES ARTS DE L'ONTARIO

Library and Archives Canada Cataloguing in Publication

Yee, Paul
    Chinatown : an illustrated history of the Chinese communities of Victoria, Vancouver, Calgary, Edmonton, Winnipeg, Toronto, Montreal and Halifax / Paul Yee.

ISBN10: 1-55028-842-3
ISBN13: 978-1-55028-842-1

1. Chinese—Canada—History.
2. Chinese Canadians—History.
3. Chinese—Canada—Social conditions.
4. Chinese Canadians—Social conditions.
I. Title.

FC106.C5Y428 2005          971'.004951          C2005-903289-8

James Lorimer & Company Ltd., Publishers
35 Britain Street
Toronto, Ontario
M5A 1R7
www. lorimer.ca

Printed and bound in China

# CONTENTS

For Daniel and Monica Mak
Stephen and Joyce —
another generation of newcomers.

DEPARTMENT OF IMMIGRATION and COLONIZATION
CHINESE
JUN 27 1924
IMMIGRATION
CANADA

# ACKNOWLEDGEMENTS

James Lorimer & Company Publishers Ltd. commissioned this book in line with its long interest in Canadian urban history, so the firm should be credited for the idea.

During text research, I was helped by Judith Fingard of Dalhousie University, Dora Nipp and the staff of the Multicultural History Society of Ontario, Judy Chan, Nancy Li, Patrick May and Larry Wong of Vancouver, and Robert Yip of Ottawa. I am indebted to archivists, librarians and inter-library loan staff at institutions across the country.

An Ontario Arts Council grant facilitated the visual research. Assistance was received from Paul Dofoo and Ray Lee in Calgary, Dorothy Choy, Ken Wong, and Dr. Joseph Du in Winnipeg, Ginette Dugas, Mary S.Y. Wong, Cynthia Lam, Pauline Wong, and Janet Lumb in Montreal, William Joe, Binglin Wong, Donald and Mabel Kwan, and King Wan Wu in Ottawa, and Doug Hum, Douglas Lee, and Keith Lock in Toronto. In Halifax, Albert Lee and Mary Mohamed provided images.

*Clown in lucky red costume teases lion dancers in a parade.*

# INTRODUCTION

Ten years before Confederation in 1867, the first few Chinese newcomers were already living and working in the territory that would become part of Canada. By the twenty-first century, the Chinese had become 3.5 percent of Canada's population, the nation's largest racial minority. Chinese was the third most spoken mother tongue in Canada, after English and French.

The Chinese prominence in Canada is recent. Hong Kong was the leading supplier of immigrants to Canada from 1987 to 1994, after which China became the top source. In some years, a quarter of all newcomers to Canada were Chinese. Most settled in the cities that had become home to long-standing Chinese communities.

This book looks at Chinatowns in eight Canadian cities, each with its own personality. Vancouver is "laid-back," while Calgary is "brash." Toronto "works too hard" and Montreal is "European." Despite local differences, however, the Chinese shared similar experiences from one city to the next. This background chapter starts with nineteenth-century peasants and ends with high-tech professionals of the postmodern world. It traces the ability of the Chinese to flourish in Canada, despite popular and legislated racism, and become full participants in a proudly multicultural nation.

## The Two Waves

One way to understand Canada's Chinese is to think of an invisible historical line running through Chinese-Canadian communities. On one side are the pre-1923 pioneers and their descendants. On the other are the post-1947 immigrants and their families, who greatly outnumber the first group. These two sides had different life experiences, yet they are often lumped into one group.

The typical pre-1923 immigrant was an uneducated male peasant from south China. His family stayed behind while he

HONGKONG.

華僑登記證 No. 3895
Certificate of Registration

*Above: Overseas immigrants passed through Hong Kong's harbour, 1900.*

*Below: Document issued by Chinese consulate in 1942 to Lee Dan May, who came to Canada in 1912 and settled in Winnipeg.*

entered a Canada that detested the Chinese. More recent Chinese immigrants, especially those who came after 1984, were families headed by persons with professional training and English language abilities. They came from modern cities in China, Southeast Asia, and around the world.

Immigrants have always been attached to their homelands, even as they became Canadians. But due to racist attitudes in Canada, the pre-1923 Chinese migrants could not obtain citizenship, so many of them planned to return to China.

Recent newcomers also kept homeland ties, but did not endure the "half-lives" (half here, half there) of earlier immigrants who yearned between two lands. They embraced two worlds, learning Canada's official languages and coping with its cold climate while maintaining contact with their motherlands. With technology beaming Asian news and entertainment into Canada and travel time to Asia greatly reduced, today's Chinese immigrants enjoy many advantages of both continents.

## An Ancient Homeland

The Chinese who journeyed to North America starting in the mid-nineteenth century came from a rural area near Guangzhou (Canton) and Hong Kong in Guangdong province. There was a long-standing culture of out-migration; men sent money home and women stayed behind to maintain families and ancient traditions. The wives of men who stayed away a long time in North America especially lamented their husbands' absence:

> *We had been wed for only a few nights;*
> *Then you left me for Gold Mountain.*
> *For twenty long years you haven't returned.*
> *For this, I embrace only resentment in my bedroom.*[1]

These migrants were peasants or hired hands, as well as peddlers and tradespeople from towns. Some owned small

*South China's warm climate allowed two crops of rice annually, but this was still insufficient to support the growing population.*

*Gold miner using shoulder pole to carry supplies, 1870s.*

plots of land; others had none. Although few spoke English and many couldn't read or write Chinese, they all possessed strong cultural values.

Family was paramount, because land and wealth were transferred within it. Families with the same surname belonged to a clan, an entity that rented out collective land, sponsored schools, and built dikes. Clan members, especially those who worked abroad, were expected to increase the clan's pooled wealth so that all members, rich and poor alike, could enjoy the clan's prestige and protection.

The primacy of family was a fundamental principle of Confucianism, which then set rules for Chinese society. Sons and daughters obeyed their parents, females submitted to males, and seniors were esteemed. Confucianism also valued book learning, which enabled men to rise above their humble origins. Any educated person who succeeded in examinations for the imperial bureaucracy could gain status and wealth. Merchants would even purchase official titles because of the respect paid to scholars.

Another value that Chinese brought with them involved free market capitalism, which flourished in China. Peasants sold produce at markets, and merchants traded across cities and regions. People raised business capital by borrowing from clans or moneylenders, or by pooling funds with others. Migrants motivated by free enterprise thinking met similar ideas in Canada.

The nineteenth century brought trouble to China. By 1850 Guangdong province had doubled its population to 28 million over a 70-year period, straining the land's ability to feed the people. Land was unequally distributed, and tenant-peasants faced high rents and taxes. Western imperialism deepened the misery as new foreign-dominated treaty ports were opened, diverting trade and jobs away from Guangzhou. And the arrival of Western machine-made textiles ruined the market for native hand-woven fabrics.

The rural crisis sparked a peasant rebellion that overran central China in the 1850s. Other uprisings in the Pearl River Delta in 1854–64 claimed 100,000 lives, while conflicts over land and water rights caused 150,000 casualties. The weakened central government could not protect peasants from bandits or relieve floods, droughts and food shortages. And the dynasty's "self-strengthening" efforts to combat the influence of the West failed, as foreign powers divided the country into "spheres of influence."

## Not Welcome Here

In British Columbia, the early Chinese, often called "sojourners," worked as gold miners, laundrymen and market gardeners. They also became teamsters, coal miners, salmon canners, and servants. Between 1881 and 1885, 17,000 Chinese arrived, many recruited expressly to help build the Canadian Pacific Railway in British Columbia. Whites there vociferously opposed using Chinese workers, but Prime Minister John A. Macdonald told them in 1882: "It is simply a question of alternatives: either you must have this labour or you can't have the railway."

About three-quarters of the labourers who worked on the British Columbia section of the railway were Chinese. Their job was to clear the path and build the roadbed. This meant cutting down trees, removing rock, clearing tunnels, and levelling the grade. Chinese workers earned a dollar a day, two-thirds of what a white man received for comparable work.

As construction on the CPR came to an end in 1885, the Chinese headed into the prairies and Ontario, and even further east to the Maritimes, seeking work. Now that imported labour was no longer needed, Canada levied a $50 head tax on Chinese newcomers, reflecting the powerful anti-Asian racism of the time.

Prevailing racist views saw China as a backward and poor country that was vastly inferior to Western nations. Chinese immigrants were seen as unclean, unhealthy, corrupted by opium and gambling, and a threat to Canada's social order. Some aspects of their immigration reinforced these fears: the mostly male nature of Chinese migrants gave rise to sexual paranoia, as white Canadians worried that Chinese men without wives would seek sex from white women. Laws in Saskatchewan (1912), Manitoba (1913), Ontario (1914), and British Columbia (1919) explicitly banned Chinese from hiring white women, in order to reduce inter-racial contact.

The trends of eastward movement and racism merged in the jobs the Chinese found (or didn't find). In Alberta, the

*1907 cartoon illustrating majority attitudes towards Asian immigration.*

Chinese laboured in mines, market gardens, laundries, and restaurants. But in the rest of Canada, they worked almost exclusively in laundries and restaurants because white employers would not hire them and because washing clothes and cooking were seen as womanly toil. Only in British Columbia

*By 1952, the women of Winnipeg's Chinese United Church included longtime wives, Canadian-born girls and reunited wives.*

did large numbers of Chinese work in industries involving agriculture, lumber, and fish. But even there white workers often lashed out at the Chinese for accepting lower wages, and thereby "stealing" work from them.

The lasting damage of racism was enshrined in Canadian immigration law. In response to pressure from labour groups and politicians in British Columbia, the head tax rose to $100 in 1900, and then to $500, an amount equal to two years' wages in 1904. Chinese immigration was banned outright in 1923, and men could no longer bring their families to Canada. They had to return to China to reunite with their loved ones. Early Chinese Canadians lived as second-class citizens subject to mob attacks or schoolboy jeers, surrounded by unfair laws and practices. Journalists and politicians, respectable men and women, labourers and captains of industry — and even chil-

dren — hurled contempt at the Chinese.

How did the Chinese respond? With dignity and carefully measured words. Won Alexander Cumyow, the first Canadian-born Chinese, put it this way in 1902:

> *This unfriendliness and want of respect has caused a feeling of want of confidence among the Chinese, and it certainly has not tended to induce them to abandon their own ways and modes of life ... My opinion is, that if the Chinese were accorded the same respect as others here, they would prove themselves to be good citizens, and they would settle in the land with their wives and families.*[2]

But the Chinese were not yet "accorded the same respect," even by the law. The justice system, from front-line police up to judges in court, shared the hostility. When law enforcers cracked down on gambling among the Chinese, Cumyow pointed to its relative innocence:

> *"There is proportionately a large amount of gambling among the Chinese. Some do gamble for large amounts, but more commonly the play is for amusement only, and for small sums to pass the time, as this is done in the common room of a boarding house, where all are assembled, though differently occupied."*[3]

Nevertheless, the Royal Commission he was addressing concluded that the Chinese were "obnoxious" and "dangerous to the state."[4]

Evangelical Christians offered help and sympathy through English classes, and some Chinese converted to Christianity, becoming lifelong church supporters. But not all Chinese changed their faith, for they saw first-hand how the biblical teachings of love and brotherhood were ignored by many white Christians.

While Chinese-Canadian history was stained by racism, dwelling on it can over-emphasize how those with power abused it. Studies of racism tend to portray Chinese as helpless victims, for they indeed lacked political power. But looking at this same dark history through the lens of Canada's vibrant Chinatowns can illumine the spirit that thrived in Chinese communities through service groups, politics, sports, and other cultural pastimes. The Chinese survived racism in part by living their lives as fully as possible.

## Self-contained, Not Close-knit

According to Confucian tradition, a clan association linked families of one surname, or those of several surnames tied through history. A district association united people hailing from the same county in China. In the absence of immigrants' families, these groups provided shelter, emergency help, leads to jobs and meeting places. They marked ancestral days and festivals, settled disputes and sent the bones of deceased members back to China. Members knew that if they died in Canada, their funerals would be properly arranged.

The Chinese Freemasons Society emerged in 1863 in the gold rush town of Barkerville. It had similar duties to clan and district groups, but also made rules for behaviour in the frontier. A fourth group was community-wide: the Chinese Benevolent Association (CBA). Its board evolved to include members from clan, district, and fraternal organizations. It settled disputes among member groups and voiced concerns to the larger society. Western reporters often called the local CBA president the "Mayor of Chinatown."

These groups shaped self-contained communities. But self-contained did not mean close-knit, because divisions based on clan, politics, education, language ability, and jobs sliced through all Chinatowns and created differing loyalties. Chinatown residents did not all think alike just because they came from the same country.

*Freemasons' lion dancers in Victoria's downtown, 1920.*

## International Politics

Like other immigrants, the Chinese avidly followed their homeland politics. They especially wanted to see China strengthened in the global arena, hoping that the sting of racism would lessen if China became a respected power. Canada's immigration policies were also affected by international power struggles.

Many blamed China's weakness on the foreign Manchu rulers. In China, scholars Liang Qichao and Kang Youwei sought to reform the state, but Western-educated Dr. Sun Yat-sen (a medical doctor) plotted revolution to establish a republic. Both Kang and Dr. Sun sought financial support abroad. Overseas merchants endorsed Kang through the Chinese Empire Reform

*Artist Sing Lim portrayed his mother working at home in Vancouver in the 1920s.*

Association (CERA), while the Chinese Freemasons raised funds for Dr. Sun.

After the Manchu Dynasty collapsed in 1911, Dr. Sun created a party, the Kuomintang (KMT), to govern China. But the fledgling democracy foundered, and civil war ensued. Dr. Sun's "southern" government rallied support from the overseas Chinese, who formed local KMT branches (also known as Chinese National Leagues) to carry out fundraising and education. The Freemasons felt that their financial support for the 1911 revolution had been ignored by the KMT in China, and a bitter rivalry sprang up between the two allegiances.

Dr. Sun failed to unify China. In 1918 Ottawa closed KMT branches throughout Canada because the southern government opposed China's northern regime, which was Britain's World War I ally against Germany. The ban lasted six months. In 1922, when China tried to negotiate trade and immigration treaties with Canada, Chinese Canadians hoped immigration would be protected. But when Canada learned that the northern regime did not control south China, source of Canada's immigrants, it ended talks. Shortly afterwards, in 1923, Chinese immigration was banned.

China's ongoing national weakness was all too apparent to Chinese around the world, including those in Canada. On May 20, 1925, workers and students in China were protesting the killing of a worker by a Japanese foreman in a Shanghai factory. British police fired on the protesters and killed twelve. This "Shanghai Incident" caused nation-wide riots and strikes against the foreign presence in China. Overseas Chinese rallied and donated funds to the cause.

China's plight as the "sick man of Asia" later helped reverse white opinions of Chinese Canadians. Japan invaded China in 1931 and World War II broke out eight years later. After the Japanese attack on Pearl Harbor, the United States entered the war. China also sided with the Allies and was seen to be fighting alongside them in Asia. Canada's Chinese supported both homelands with fundraising, and 500 Chinese Canadians enlisted in Canada's armed forces. The tide of racism had begun to turn.

**Towards Integration**

After the war, the exclusion law was repealed, and the Chinese-Canadian community began to grow again as residents with Canadian citizenship brought over their wives and children. Canadian-born Chinese found new options when racial barriers were dropped and voting rights were granted. They began moving into homes in better districts, and a generation of Chinese-Canadian baby-boomers was born.

In China the civil war resumed. In 1949, when the Communists established the People's Republic of China, the KMT set up a government-in-exile on the island of Taiwan. During the Cold War, China was shut out of international affairs as Taiwan held China's seat at the United Nations. Chinese communities across North America embraced Taiwan as the rightful government of all of China.

The Communists seized the lands and wealth of south China's immigrant families, terrorizing them during land reform. They also attacked two pillars of Chinese tradition, Confucianism and capitalism. Overseas Chinese gave up their dreams of retiring in China and resigned themselves to life abroad. Unfortunately, Canadian laws continued to prevent relatives in China from joining them.

The pressure to escape Mainland China was enormous. It spawned an industry of forging documents to create "slots" in existing Chinese-Canadian families for overseas clients. In 1960 the police raided Chinatowns across Canada, trying to stem the illegal movement. Two years later, the Canadian government's Chinese Adjustment Statement Program permitted migrants to come forth to remedy their status without being prosecuted. Over the next decade, 12,000 Chinese took advantage of this amnesty.

When Canada proposed diplomatic ties with China in the 1960s, Taiwan's KMT allies in Chinatowns opposed such moves. The struggle between KMT supporters and opponents continued into the 1980s, as those trying to discredit people and groups who favoured closer contact with Mainland China would label them Communists.

### Crossroads

By the 1960s, the story of Chinese Canadians resembled that of other immigrants to Canada. A first generation had struggled against physical hardships. A second generation grew up between motherland and Canadian cultures, not fully at home in either, because of language difficulties and racism. After World War II an era of tolerance and acceptance emerged. For Chinese Canadians, equality seemed within reach; it seemed possible to join the mainstream.

Chinese immigration suddenly resumed, and newcomers made Chinese communities very visible again. They revitalized the declining Chinatowns, which had become powerful symbols of cultural difference.

The 1960s Chinatowns still had active community groups. The pre-1923 old-timers controlled traditional organizations. The "re-unifieds" were their offspring, who had been born in China and arrived as teenagers after 1947. By the 1960s they had families, owned businesses, or worked in service and technical fields. And they joined their fathers' associations. A few Canadian-born Chinese also worked in Chinatowns. As well, it was the location of Chinese schools for baby-boomer children.

When urban renewal threatened Canada's Chinatowns

*1950's football star Normie Kwong was appointed Alberta's Lieutenant-Governor in 2005.*

each in turn, much demolition occurred before Chinese Canadians fought back. Ultimately, as the images here illustrate, Canada's Chinatowns revived and flourished, thanks to renewed immigration. Demands for homeland foods and products brought an economic boom as new stores and services such as video outlets and radio programs appeared. Chinese-speaking doctors, lawyers, and accountants practised in Chinatown alongside immigrant-aid agencies.

## Dynamic Homelands

Immigration law has always shaped Chinese-Canadian communities. In 1967 Ottawa issued one set of entry rules for applicants from all countries, and Chinese could finally enter on their own merits. The new rules favoured people who spoke an official language, had higher education, and held the job skills needed. In the mid-1980s, Canada set up entry categories to attract business talent and investment capital. The Entrepreneur class admitted people who had a successful business record as well as a plan to create jobs in Canada. Investor class immigrants had to be personally worth $500,000 and place at least $250,000 in venture funds of high-risk capital.

The first wave of Chinese migrants had come from one small region in China, but their successors hailed from cities in Africa, South America and Southeast Asia. Most came from Hong Kong, Taiwan and China.

## Hong Kong

In 1967 strikes, riots and bombings suddenly paralyzed Hong Kong. Across the border, Chairman Mao had launched his Cultural Revolution, unleashing Red Guards to challenge all authority. This show of power caused many Hong Kong residents to emigrate. Even more departed after the 1972 stock market crash and after 1986, when billionaire Li Ka-shing sig-

nalled his confidence in Canada.

At the time, Hong Kong was a stunning Asian success story. In the decades after 1949 its people had transformed a patch of land with no natural resources (except a harbour) into the world's third-largest financial centre (after New York and London) and the world's third-largest container port. Refugees from China continually boosted the labour supply and the consumer market. As well, Hong Kong's devotion to a free market spurred business growth.

Countless "rags-to-riches" stories inspired residents to start businesses, and small to medium-sized, family-owned firms dominated Hong Kong. The hundreds of thousands of refugees were frugal and thrifty, and they worked steadily. Hong Kong had a small wealthy elite, a huge pool of labour and a growing middle class, all of whom believed that hard work led to success.

The handover to China occurred peacefully. Hong Kong's stocks and housing prices soared in 1997, luring back many ex-residents from Canada. Vancouver was affected most by this movement, as real estate prices in the high-end west side fell by an estimated 20 percent. However, a devastating currency crisis and economic slump in Asia pricked Hong Kong's bubble, and it began to decline, partly as a result also of Shanghai's rise as China's commercial centre. Immigrants in Canada with significant investments in Hong Kong felt the impact of this downturn on their income.

## Taiwan

Taiwan was another Asian economic miracle that was nervously tied to events in China. After martial law ended in Taiwan in 1987, a democracy emerged. In 1996, during Taiwan's first elections, Beijing fired unarmed missiles off the coast. Taiwanese politicians campaigned for the island's independence, but China wanted it "reunified" with the mainland. This unease,

*Hong Kong's overcrowding was one factor causing immigrants to leave.*

along with the lifting of foreign exchange controls, caused many Taiwanese to emigrate.

Thanks to Taiwan's strong economy, many citizens left as Independent and Business class immigrants. After World War II, low-cost labour had made the island a key textile exporter and producer of cars, machinery, ships and petrochemicals. In 2000, it made half the world's notebook computers, monitors, motherboards and scanners. As in Hong Kong, the government of Taiwan was laissez-faire about regulating businesses, allowing hundreds of small and medium-sized family companies to flourish.

## China

Three years after Canada and China established diplomatic ties in 1970, the two signed an agreement to permit family reunification. Over 30,000 Mainland Chinese came to Canada between 1973 and 1988.

Chinese immigration jumped again after the 1989 Tiananmen Square crackdown. Chinese nationals in Canada received "sympathetic evaluations" of their immigrant status, and many students, visiting scholars, contract workers and visitors decided to stay on. In the following year, 8000 received landed status and started sponsoring family members to join them.

The fact that Mainlanders were in Canada in 1989 reflected a decade of dramatic change in China. To increase productivity, China purchased foreign technology and sent citizens abroad to study. To free the economy from state control, the government let marketplaces thrive and set up Special Economic Zones to attract overseas investment. In the 1980s China's economic growth averaged 10 percent a year, but living standards lagged behind those of Hong Kong and Taiwan.

After upheavals such as the Cultural Revolution and the

*The Tiananmen Square incident provoked protests in many cities, including Montreal, 1989.*

Great Leap Forward, China's people supported the shift towards personal profit. The wealthy bought cars and modern appliances. But economic growth slowed in the late 1990s as massive layoffs hit state-owned enterprises.

After Canada started processing immigrants in China itself in 1995, the country soon became the top source of migrants to Canada. Many qualified as Skilled Workers (previously classed as Independent immigrants); later, others would come as Business immigrants. Many left China because of its police state, one-child policy, over-population, and lack of freedom and opportunity.

As well, the people in China, Taiwan and Hong Kong had become weary of pollution, overcrowding, corruption, crime, and the pressures of gaining university admission. But they were proud of the thriving economies and cultures of their

## Newcomers and New Issues

Once the difficult decision to leave one's homeland and one's familiar world had been made, the difficulties of resettlement needed to be faced. Immigrants without official language skills or higher education (refugees, for example) landed in low-paying jobs with little future. They placed their hopes in their children, vowing, "We'll tough it out, so our children won't have to."

Better-qualified immigrants resettled more easily. But professionals were dismayed when licensing bodies rejected their credentials, or when employers demanded "Canadian experience" or perfect English. As for Entrepreneur class migrants, they had to have a new business up and running in two years. This was hardly enough time for them to make local contacts and learn about new markets and laws. Some set up mainstream firms, while others undertook Chinese-centred businesses and travelled between Canada and Asia to manage imports, exports and factories.

Other immigrants also travelled frequently. Business people and professionals knew their incomes would drop after they arrived in Canada. In order to maintain their lifestyle, these migrants decided (reversing the pattern of the first Chinese immigrants) that one spouse, usually the wife, would live in Canada with the children, while the other worked in Asia. The amount of time they spent flying back and forth across the Pacific Ocean earned them the label of "astronauts."

Most immigrants headed to cities where jobs and Chinatowns beckoned. Groups providing Chinese-language counselling turned into formal agencies with high-profile board members, accredited social workers and bilingual/trilingual workers. They served seniors, troubled teenagers, families, the unemployed, potential entrepreneurs and others in need. Their funds came from the three levels of government and

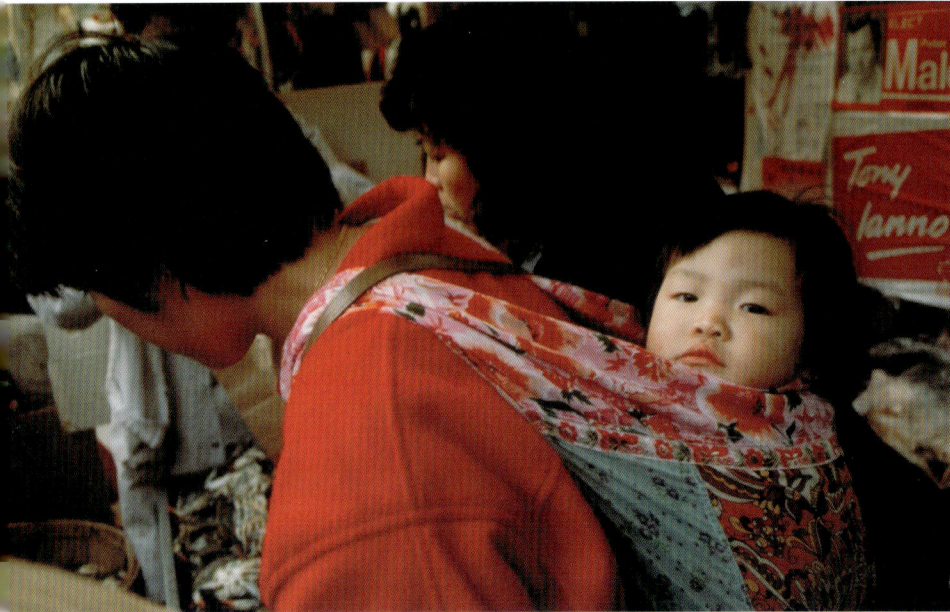

*Chinese immigrants want their children to grow up speaking English or French.*

homelands, and confident in their personal abilities in the modern economy.

Southeast Asia was another major source of Chinese migrants to Canada. Although the Chinese were a minority in the region, their successes had long provoked envy from native populations. Singapore had risen as a largely Chinese city-state in 1963 to defy the Malay majority in Malaysia. In 1969 mobs rampaged through Chinese districts in Kuala Lumpur, killing and looting. Several thousand Chinese Indonesians were killed after the 1965 coup, and violence continued into the next decade. In the Philippines the Chinese were affected by martial law in 1972. And, after America withdrew from Vietnam, Canada accepted 60,000 Indo-Chinese refugees from Vietnam, Cambodia and Laos.

donations by mainstream and Chinese communities.

Although Canada's laws banned racism and a multiculturalism policy encouraged diversity, three racial issues re-emerged in the 1970s. Ottawa's 1975 Green Paper on Immigration was supposed to start discussions on immigration options, but ethnic groups denounced it for blaming unemployment, urban housing shortages and social tensions on immigrants.

In 1979 the CTV-W5 program "Campus Giveaway" alleged that foreign students were squeezing Canadian students out of universities. Each time the narrator mentioned foreign students, Chinese faces were shown. In fact, these faces belonged to Canadians either born here or landed as citizens. The message that Chinese people could never become Canadians provoked a cross-country protest until CTV was forced to apologize.

When the 1979–80 "Boat People" brought refugees from the Vietnam area wars to Canada, half of Canadians felt the government was accepting too many refugees, and strident letters to newspapers across the country trumpeted this message.

In the mid-1980s anti-Chinese sentiments surfaced in cities with high immigration. The mainstream media claimed that Asian money was driving up real estate costs, especially in Vancouver. Those who disliked what they termed the "selling" of Canadian passports to Investor immigrants denigrated them. And Chinese newcomers learned belatedly that their determination to work hard was seen by some as "too materialistic."

**New Vision**

Contemporary Chinese-Canadian communities are keen on homeland news and politics, just as they had earlier been passionate about modernizing China in the 1890s or supporting China's war against Japan. Friends, relatives and business associates in their former countries make homeland connections highly personal as well.

*Dragon boat racing is popular across Canada and internationally.*

Many Chinese in Canada have business ties to China. Governments here seek increased trade with China and hope immigrants can help in bringing the two sides together. Other homeland ties have been less well received. For example, when immigrants from China celebrated Beijing's win of the 2008 Olympic Games over Toronto, they were reproached for a lack of loyalty to Canada.

Over the years, Chinatowns have changed from being needed to being optional. Chinese Canadians no longer needed a zone of safety, except for seniors who didn't speak English, and most Chinese Canadians no longer lived or worked near old Chinatowns. However, newcomers enjoyed meeting friends, receiving settlement services, and buying familiar goods in the "old" and "new" Chinatowns that were commercial districts or malls.

Some Chinese saw old Chinatowns as living monuments to a turbulent history and to the fragility of equality. Others saw them as sites where Chinese culture was preserved and shared. Both these views supported the building of cultural facilities there. In a sense, old and new Chinatowns bridged the historical divide between Chinese Canadians, because more and more people appreciated Chinatowns' different functions and freely visited them.

In all cities, cultural activities developed that were available to Chinese and non-Chinese alike. Some aspects reflected Western interest in acupuncture, martial arts and tai-chi. Other aspects reflected Chinese Canadians' desire to retain their heritage, especially around language. Converging interests were highlighted in events such as dragon boat races, held in almost every city in this book. The races are centuries old but now include teams from all parts of Canadian society, including corporations, cancer survivors, high school students, and serious rowers. Some winning teams attend international races in Asia.

This trend towards integration was buttressed by the ongoing participation of Chinese Canadians in mainstream Canadian arts and politics. Stories of Chinese Canadians became seen as Canadian stories; elected officials strove to serve all their constituents. As W.A. Cumyow predicted over a century ago, the Chinese have proved themselves to be good citizens.

Throughout Canada, Chinatowns are woven into the urban fabric. Those in Victoria and Vancouver contain historic buildings; those in Calgary and Winnipeg have cultural centres that are showcase attractions. In some cities, the push to revitalize downtown cores was helped by Chinese seniors who moved to Chinatowns. In all cities, Chinatowns testify at the very least to the viability of diversity.

*Chinatowns are busy shopping districts that also support cultural activities.*

# *1*

# VICTORIA: THE WESTERN FRONTIER

If you take the Chinatown tour in Victoria, the two highlights can seem worlds apart. The Gate of Harmonious Interest from 1981 is an extravaganza of Chinese design featuring yellow roof tiles, wooden brackets painted blue and white, mythical creatures and a flourish of Chinese calligraphy. It arches over Fisgard Street, where the lack of traffic gives it a graceful air.

Nearby Fan Tan Alley is a long, dark pathway between brick buildings that block out

*The Gate of Harmonious Interest, and entrance to Victoria's Chinatown, 1981.*

the sunlight. In some places it is only four feet wide. It dates from the early 1900s and has an exotic history. The alley was popular among gamblers, because of its many eateries and gamehouses. Wooden doors used to seal the lane, and guards peered through peepholes before admitting people.

The contrast between these two spots reminds us that this colourful and quaint area was once very different. Canada's first Chinatown, and the nation's largest for fifty years, grew up in Victoria, when it was a port for gold miners and railway navvies. Since then, other cities have attracted Chinese Canadians and nurtured Chinatowns far larger and busier, but none can rival Victoria's place as Canada's oldest Chinatown and, as of 1996, a "Canadian Heritage District."

### New World Opportunities

The early Chinese immigrants were of two classes: workers, who took many demanding and harsh jobs throughout the frontier; and merchants, who supplied them with goods and services, and acted as community leaders.

In 1858, when rumours of gold along the Fraser River reached San Francisco, the Chinese there dispatched one man north to check the situation. The scout returned to tell of miners scrambling for the precious ore. Within a few months, 20,000 people had thronged through Fort Victoria, the fur trading post on "Vancouver's Island," heading for the mainland. In response to this sudden influx, Britain quickly claimed the mainland as a crown colony (British Columbia) in order to maintain British rule against growing numbers of American miners.

Among the early arrivals to Victoria in 1858 was Chang Tsoo, owner of Yang Wo Sang, a large San Francisco company. When his countrymen followed eagerly, Chang provided them with shelter, provisions and mining equipment.

Chang's competitors were Lee Chong and the Loo brothers of the Kwong Lee Company, and the Tai Soong Company (the former firm based in San Francisco, the latter in Hong Kong). In boomtown Victoria, Chinese merchants also invested in real estate. Seven of them purchased land near the harbour (where five-dollar lots had suddenly jumped to $500 or $1000), but Chang Tsoo and a Loo brother invested downtown. Their holdings became Canada's first Chinatown.[1]

More Chinese kept coming. Among the 4000 arrivals of 1860 were Lee Chong's wife and two children, the first Chinese family in Victoria. Chinese from Hong Kong or China had no mining experience, unlike those from California. By then, six or seven thousand Chinese were prospecting for gold in British Columbia.[2]

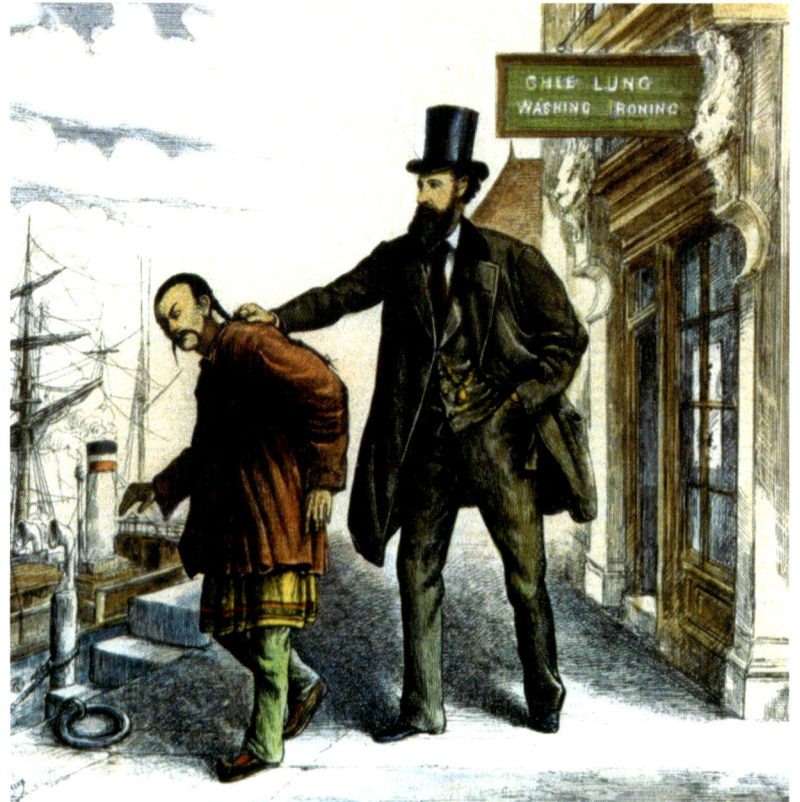

*Politician scolds a Chinese: "You won't drink whiskey, talk politics and vote like us." (1879).*

One 1862 tally counted 300 Chinese in Victoria. This number rose whenever a ship arrived, and then dropped as the migrant workers left for the mainland. The Chinese lived both inside and outside Chinatown. The former included woodcutters, hotel cooks, peddlers, merchants and shopkeepers (cobblers, barbers, herbalists and tailors), who helped miners get ready for their trek. Market gardeners, laundry-men and servants lived on their farms and stores or in the homes of their well-to-do employers.

Victoria thrived as mainland resources were exploited. The gold rushes spread north to the Cariboo and east to the Kootenays in the 1860s, providing a variety of jobs for the Chinese. A thousand of them earned $40 a month building a wagon road to the north. In New Westminster, they constructed dikes and dug ditches, and strung 660 kilometres of telegraph wires to Quesnel in the north. In gold rush towns, they were laundrymen, cooks and market gardeners. In 1866, they started working in coal mines as well.

Chinatown's merchants booked ships to transport the migrants and housed them when they arrived. They imported Chinese food and distributed it throughout British Columbia via branch stores. In small towns, these branches sent migrants' money back to China for them, and stored their in-bound

*1880 view of building erected by Loo Chew Fan on Cormorant Street.*

*Above: Immigrants wore traditional clothes for portraits to send home, c1890.*
*Below: Worker at the Victoria Rice Mill, 1889.*

mail. Staff would read letters to illiterate men and draft replies as needed.

In Victoria, merchants were community leaders. On one occasion they told a reporter to expect 10,000 Chinese in 1860, leaving the newspaper to speculate how increased traffic could possibly benefit the city![3] When a new governor arrived, the merchants donated $103 to the welcome committee. Chang Tsoo and Lee Chong came to meet him with a translator and expressed their support for British rule, which was "so reverse" to that in California. The merchants were bullish about prospects:

> *The maritime enterprise will add up wonderfully and come quick. China has silks, tea, rice, sugar, &c. Here is lumber, coal and minerals, in return, and fish an exhaustless supply, which no other land can surpass.*[4]

Victoria continued to thrive in the 1880s when the CPR used Chinese workers for railway construction. The recruiting and transport companies Lian Chang, Tai Yuan and Guang An Lung operated from Victoria. Chinese also found other jobs in the city. By 1884 there were 130 boot makers, 114 vegetable farmers, 65 woodcutters, 60 brick makers, 36 peddlers, 30 seamsters, 28 cigar makers and 12 doctors.

One penniless but enterprising Chinese who reached Victoria in 1870 heard of peddlers buying herring from fishermen for 25 cents and then selling it at 75 cents. The man sold some medicine to get 25 cents. Then he bought some fish and sold it. Soon he earned enough to start a small store selling tobacco and matches to First Nations people. They in turn convinced him to trade with other First Nations villages. So the man bought groceries from the Hudson's Bay Company, loaded them onto a boat, and headed up the coast. In his last job before returning to China, he delivered cordwood to Victoria on his boat.[5]

## Life Was Hard

In their non-work time, Victoria's Chinese could gamble, learn English at the Methodist mission, visit one of nine Chinatown brothels, seek guidance from the God of Seafarers at the Tam Kung Temple or join the Chinese Freemasons, formed locally in 1876. They were not likely to stay at home because living conditions were wretched. As workers flooded into town, shelter was in short supply, and men had to crowd into dirt-floored cabins amidst garbage-strewn alleys. There were no sidewalks, sewers or running water.[6] Newcomers camped on vacant lots.

Racism took many forms in the early British Columbia context. In 1865 Chinese merchants had to pay $100 for a licence to sell opium, while white druggists were exempt because they "prescribed" it as medicine.[7] When gold mining collapsed and the economy slowed down in the 1870s, racism became more strident. Victoria's Workingman's Protective Association in 1878 boycotted firms that hired Chinese workers, and asked Ottawa to restrict Chinese immigration. British Columbia banned Chinese from public works and levied a head tax of $60 on them, but Chinese merchants successfully petitioned federal authorities to disallow the tax.

Bleak conditions prompted merchants to form the Chinese Consolidated Benevolent Association (CCBA) in 1884. They told the Chinese Consul-General how "gangs of vicious Chinese were bullying their fellow-countrymen; the old, the poor and the unemployed suffered from coldness, sickness and starvation, and some had died in the streets; prostitution, gambling, brawling, fighting, intimidation and extortion pervaded the Chinese communities."[8] In the previous year, great numbers of Chinese discharged from railway work had landed penniless in Victoria.

*Above: Women and children at church gathering, 1902.*
*Below: Peddler in Gordon Head, 1908.*

*Watercolour painting of Chinese farm, by Josephine Crease, 1913.*

The CCBA opposed discriminatory laws and instituted rules of conduct for the Chinese in Canada. For example, any Chinese victimized by a Westerner could seek help from the association. Any girl sold in Victoria was to be handed to the benevolent group for return to Hong Kong.[9] The CCBA returned destitute workers to China and maintained a cemetery. When joblessness and racism peaked, it sent notices to China advising against immigration. A 1899 letter described many difficulties:

> The cost of living in a foreign country is very high … ten times as much as … in China. The minimum expenditure per capita is five to six dollars per month or between sixty to seventy dollars per year. Therefore the annual income of ten to twenty dollars cannot cover the expense.
>
> If you … are determined to come, you should bring along with you some extra money … to pay for your board and lodging while you are still seeking work. Otherwise, you will find yourself in a terrible plight and have to sleep in the open with no job, no food, and no salvation.[10]

In the 1890s the Chinese sank deeper roots into Victoria. They demolished Chinatown's wooden shacks and erected brick buildings. Merchants created a Chinese Chamber of Commerce in 1893, and built a Chinese hospital. For the community's 100 children, the CCBA opened a Chinese school in 1899. By 1902 ten district associations had been founded.

## School Segregation

One long-standing issue pitted the city's Chinese, their compatriots across Canada, and China's government against the local school board. In 1903 the Victoria School Board became the only one in Canada to segregate Chinese students

*Chinese Public School graduates, 1915.*

from their white classmates. Anti-Chinese groups had pressed for this separation, and the Chinese resisted, so children, parents, government officials and the general public became involved.[11]

In 1901 only 15 Chinese children attended classes at Rock Bay Elementary, the school closest to Chinatown. When white parents demanded that those students be placed in a separate school, teachers defended the Chinese students' diligence and good behaviour. The school board held its ground.

The parents approached the Victoria Trades and Labour Council (TLC), representing 25 unions, to raise the issue again. When provincial officials advised that segregated schools should

Victoria Chinese Freemasons receipt, 1922. Earlier, they raised $12,000 for Dr. Sun Yat-sen's revolution.

not be based on race, the school board took no action. But that autumn, city council sided with the TLC. The school board then placed Rock Bay's junior Chinese pupils in a separate classroom, but allowed older Chinese to mix at other schools.

The segregation issue incensed Chinese parents because white youngsters frequently attacked their children. Schoolgirls complained that boys threw stones at them, pulled their hair and pushed them to the ground. In one case, a boy fleeing white attackers lost a leg when a streetcar ran over him. In court, the attackers' parents agreed to damages of $250. The Chinese accepted the inadequate amount, and proceedings were stayed. When the parents refused to pay, the case went to court again. This time the judge acquitted the accused.[12]

Even the Colonist newspaper deplored the situation:

*On Sunday afternoon last about 4 o'clock a little Chinese boy, carrying a school bag containing some fruit and a pair of rubbers was assaulted by several large boys at the corner of Johnson and Blanchard Streets. He was most unmercifully beaten and the bag and its contents thrown into the mud and destroyed. Two men standing near did not interfere, but looked calmly on at the cowardly act, which was little better than highway robbery. The police were notified, but nothing further has been heard about it. If boys are encouraged to wantonly assault Chinese in this way one of these days, as a result there will be a dead Chinaman or white boy.[13]*

The school issue arose again in 1907, with a new focus. Federal law had allowed Chinese immigrant children a refund of the head tax if they attended school for a year after arriving. Few such newcomers applied for this refund until 1903, when the head tax rose from $100 to $500. The school board argued that such increased attendance wasted tax dollars, and barred Chinese children who lacked basic English skills.

The CCBA's lawyer reminded the school board that French-Canadian children with no English skills were never rejected; Victoria's Chinese paid school taxes like other citizens, and Chinese students learned quickly. The arguments fell on deaf ears. The CCBA filed a civil suit but lost when the plaintiff's father left town. In the meantime, the CCBA itself started English classes for barred students.

In 1908 the Victoria school board instituted a new test of English-language ability. Fifty-four Canadian-born Chinese passed, but 35 immigrant children did not. The school board then started partial segregation by putting all Chinese students in grades one to four in a leased space. Then the board ruled that no boy over age 10 could attend primary grades because such children were suspected of going to school only to be eligible for the head tax refund. The board also pressured Ottawa to rule in 1911 that only university students had the right to pursue the refund.

## Growing Up and Flying

Victoria attracted many political figures from China. Reformer Kang Youwei came and, during a year's stay in 1899, set up the Chinese Empire Reform Association (CERA). Dr. Sun Yat-sen visited in 1897, 1910 and 1911. The city's Chinese Freemasons raised $12,000 for his revolution.

In 1910 there were 150 families in the Chinese community of 3500. Chinatown occupied six city blocks and sold many goods and services. Canadian-born Chinese came of age between two cultures. Their Chinese Young Men's Progress Party pressed for a library and denounced gambling. Their Chinese Canadian Club was duly recognized by Chinatown's establishment. A 1909 Chinese athletic club had 90 members, while a football team had 14 players.

In supporting China's revolution, Canadian-born interests merged with those of compatriots who had left China at a young age. After the 1911 revolution, the Kuomintang (KMT) sponsored the *New Republic* newspaper in Victoria. Ongoing unrest in China caused military units to form across Canada, including Victoria. Men from these units left for China in 1916. Some returned in 1917; others joined Dr. Sun's government in the south of China. That year, businessmen Chan Dun and Lee Kwong Yee started a flying school in Victoria to train pilots for China. Five years later, Saskatoon's Keng Wah Aviation School moved to Victoria. Ten pilots, including Lee Joe and Hip Quong, were trained and went on to fly 16,000 miles and 750 flights without any accidents.

Community politics were sometimes violently played out. In 1918 a suspected KMT member shot and killed a visiting politician from China's northern government. Violence broke out between the KMT and the Freemasons in 1928 over funding for the CCBA and the Chinese Hospital.[14] Ultimately, neutral parties intervened to keep the peace.

*Chinese United Church 50th anniversary, 1935.*

The first Chinese-run greenhouse opened in 1913 and a Chinese wholesale and retail produce outlet appeared the next year. More Chinese went into the business, and by 1925 they ran 158 greenhouses covering in total 655,000 square feet, compared to the 567,000 square feet of 256 white-run greenhouses. This tough business faced high wages, unpredictable prices, the costs of heating and repairing greenhouses, and stiff competition from imported produce.[15]

## What Crimes Have I Committed?

When immigrants arrived, they were held for health checks at an immigration building near the docks. If large numbers of

*Canadian-born Edward Chow trained with volunteers at Commando Bay in B.C. to fight behind enemy lines in Southeast Asia during World War Two.*

newcomers arrived at the same time, their stay was prolonged. During such occasions Chinese carved poems and other writings on the building walls:

> *Leaving my parents, wife and children, I have come to the Gold Mountain because I am poor. By various means, I managed to gather a thousand and some odd dollars and bought my passage to Canada. Unexpectedly I was confined in the Customs Office where I was subjected to a medical checkup. They examined my eyes, forced me to strip to the waist and take off my pants to lay bare my body. What crimes have I committed? Why am I confined here like a prisoner? Sitting alone in the cell, I always think of my parents. My dear fellow countrymen, work hard here! After you are financially successful, return to your motherland and help build your mother country strong and rich.*[16]

In 1921 the school issue focused on public health. The Chamber of Commerce was agitating against Chinese-owned grocery stores and re-activated the segregation issue when four chamber members joined the school board. When they claimed Chinese homes were unclean, the city's health office supported the Chinese and refuted the charge.

In 1922 the trustees decided to segregate the city's 216 Chinese students. The CCBA, Chinese Chamber of Commerce and Chinese Canadian Club protested in vain. Then, on the first day of school, as Chinese students were being escorted to a segregated site, they suddenly scattered. They went on strike, led by the CCBA's Anti-Segregation Association (ASA).

The ASA urged Chinese parents to boycott the segregated schools, and inspected them to ensure compliance. It sought support from business and education groups in China, and from Chinese communities across Canada. Over $16,000 was raised. In October, the school board warned that if students didn't report to the segregated sites within four days, the school term would be ended. When the strike continued, the trustees suspended all 200 students.

In response, the ASA opened a Chinese Free School. Chinese ratepayers and sympathetic whites signed a petition and the Consul-General brought in China's support. But the strike went to the end of the school term.

Finally, the next September, the school board relented, and most Chinese pupils returned to their original schools. But partial segregation continued: all the Chinese students in one district had to attend Rock Bay Elementary until after World War II.

**High Stakes in Wartime**

The community worried about China as reports of bloodshed recurred. In 1925, after the "Shanghai Incident," 600 people crowded into Victoria's CCBA headquarters to call for a boycott of British goods. When Japan invaded China in 1931, another mass meeting at the CCBA formed the "Resist Japan and Save the Nation" group. It sent $4000 to Chinese troops fighting in Manchuria, and the following year, raised $20,000 for the armies defending Shanghai.

Meanwhile, a Chinese Relief Room provided two meals daily to destitute men. Mrs. R.B. Mosher at first funded the operation herself, but later received government help.

After the Sino-Japanese War erupted in 1937, protests turned violent. In August 1939, Chinese and whites picketed the docks where scrap iron was being loaded for Japan. A Chinese girl leapt at one truck, forcing it to stop. Then a Chinese man jumped on another truck and grabbed the steering wheel. The truck veered across the road, hitting a picketer before the driver fled. The crowd then tossed all the iron onto the road.[17]

During the war, Victoria's 3000 Chinese raised $750,000 for China's war effort against Japan. Although they were less than 10 percent of Canada's Chinese, they purchased 20 percent of all bond purchases, and the government praised them four times.

Victoria's Chinatown contained many families whose offspring volunteered for military service. In 1940 Victoria-born Kam Len Douglas Sam tried to join the Royal Canadian Air Force but learned that volunteers had to be European. When the rules changed in 1942, he enlisted and trained at Lethbridge, Montreal and Quebec City. After earning his wings in 1943, Sergeant Sam was posted to England and flew raids on Frankfurt, Berlin, Essen, Nuremberg and Cologne. He was

*Theatre Alley looked dilapidated in 1959.*

promoted to Pilot Officer, and bombed targets in Belgium and France after D-Day. On one mission, Sam's aircraft was hit and the crew bailed out. On the ground, Sam contacted the French Resistance and joined the Free French network. France later awarded him a medal for leading Resistance fighters in repelling a German attack in Rheims.[18]

### The Changing Face of Chinatown

After the war, with the new *Canadian Citizenship Act*, Canada's Chinese won the right to vote. But despite the new status of the old-timer Chinese, Victoria's Chinatown went into decline. Earlier in the 1920s and 1930s, properties had been lost

*Fan Tan Alley before its redevelopment in 1977.*

through mortgage defaults or tax sales. While residents raised funds for the war, the number of businesses dropped from 85 in 1934 to 63 in 1947[19]; during peacetime, still more closed. Clan and district groups dissolved because of lack of members,[20] and the CCBA relinquished responsibilities such as the Chinese Hospital and bone shipments. New groups such as the Chinese Girls' Drill Team, the Chinese Golf Club and the Chinatown Lions Club reflected the interests of the younger Canadian-born Chinese, who were more integrated into the mainstream.

In 1951 Victoria's Chinese dropped to 1900 people, its lowest level in 60 years, as the pioneers died and young people moved away. In the next two decades the Chinese community gained only 200 people, even as immigration from Hong Kong and Taiwan revived other Chinatowns in Canada.

As early as 1959 city officials proposed making Chinatown a tourist attraction. This plan stalled, but the Centennial Square project of 1962 ate up Chinatown's oldest section. Other proposals for a paint-up campaign (1964), Fan Tan Alley revival (1972), or a Chinese cultural centre (1971, 1975) also stalled.

A newspaper article, "Requiem for Chinatown" noted, "The Chinese presence on Fisgard and Herald Streets decreases visibly by the year. The Tongs, a few restaurants, and three or four shops and tenement buildings are the tattered skeletal survival [of] a once-vibrant and colourful past."[21]

Chinatown's revival began in 1978, when the city asked University of Victoria geography professor David Lai for help. He proposed a comprehensive development plan that included street beautification, a Chinese gate, a care facility, subsidized housing, a renewal of Fan Tan Alley, and a community centre.

Tourism was key to Victoria, so the plan proceeded. The gate was built in 1981 from funds raised jointly by Chinese and non-Chinese. Then came new lampposts, sidewalks and signage. The

Victoria Chinatown Care Centre, a 30-bed care facility opened in 1982. Artists set up workshops in Fan Tan Alley. To help anchor a resident community, an apartment block for moderate-income renters was built in 1984. Even then, the care centre admitted white patients because there weren't enough Chinese to fill the beds.[22] The Chinese school was deemed a heritage building in 1988, and Chinatown was designated a historic district of national and architectural significance in 1996 because of its well-preserved nineteenth-century streetscapes.

New organizations undertook initiatives. In 1991 local businesspeople formed the Victoria Chinese Commerce Association (VCCA) to promote Chinatown and Chinese trade, and to help immigrant entrepreneurs. It brought the dragon boat races to Victoria in 1994.

In 1996 the Chinese cemetery at Harling Point was named a national historic site. The site by the ocean has very auspicious feng shui aspects because Gonzales Hill rises behind it, there are rocky outcroppings along the sides, and water moves below. The CCBA had established this seaside graveyard in 1903 and temporarily stored bones exhumed from across Canada there. But war and the rise of Communism halted bone shipments to China. In 1990, when the CCBA tried to build houses on parts of the site, neighbours protested because they feared losing their ocean views. This was ironic because earlier residents had complained that the cemetery threatened property values. When the local government zoned the site for cemetery use only, the CCBA challenged it in court. But the preservation zoning prevailed and family members continue to pay their respects there.

Despite renewal efforts, Chinatown and the downtown continued to decline. In 1997 many of Chinatown's 60 business owners hoped a Chinese-themed casino might draw customers to the area. Other Chinese Canadians were opposed:

*Chinese Public School, designated a Heritage Site in 1988, shown in 1981.*

"If we have a casino in Chinatown it would only reinforce the myth that the Chinese are inveterate gamblers." At the same time, a banker expressed concern that a casino would degrade a safe and hospitable city: "It is a very harmonious town. But once they put [a casino] in, it is going to destroy that element.[23] This opposition won the day.

**What We're Made Up Of**

In 1999 Victoria elected its first mayor of Chinese descent, Alan Lowe, an architect born and raised in the city. His regional predecessors were mayor Ed Lum of Saanich (1974–77) and mayor Harry Chow of Colwood (1988). In Oak Bay–Gordon

Head, Ida Chong was one of the first Chinese Canadian women to enter the provincial legislature in 1996.

In 1999 Victoria's Chinese were abruptly reminded of their city's historic role as a port of entry when four boats carrying 590 Chinese from Fujian province landed in British Columbia. Some 250 travellers from the first two boats were taken to a nearby military base where they applied for refugee status. Victoria's Chinese reacted in different ways. One CCBA official said, "These illegal immigrants just make the Chinese community look bad. They are giving us a negative image. I feel strongly they should be sent back. Charter a plane and send them back."[24] Another CCBA official called for compassion: "Canada is a multicultural country. That's what we're made up of. Each and every one of us, unless we're First Nation, was an immigrant of some sort."[25]

Similar reactions came from Chinese communities across Canada, but two Vancouver groups, Direct Action Against Refugee Exploitation and the Vancouver Association of Chinese Canadians, rallied behind the undocumented migrants and criticized the government. They claimed that the migrants were detained because criminal characteristics were imputed to them but not to other refugees.

By 2001 Victoria's Chinese population of 11,240 was one of the smallest in Canada, amounting to only 4 percent of city residents. Yet the city's racial mix put the Chinese at 41 percent of its visible minorities, the largest single group. Migrants from Mainland China accounted for almost 10 percent of all 1990s immigrants, ahead of those from Taiwan and Hong Kong.

Victoria also had the highest percentage of Canadian-borns, 43 percent of the city's Chinese. Recent immigration from Asia had indeed bypassed the city. When Ida Chong visited Vancouver in 1997, she commented, "I felt like I was in another country when I was in that Chinatown."[26]

*Chinese Cemetery at Harling Point, 1981.*

# *2*

# VANCOUVER: ON THE EDGE

At the end of the twentieth century, Vancouver was the most Asian of Canadian cities. It bustled with settled communities from China, Japan, Korea, South and Southeast Asia. Students from these regions flocked there to learn English, and Asian cuisine was widely available and popular. The urban landscape featured Chinatowns and Chinese malls, as well as Buddhist temples, mosques and Sikh temples. This sudden, recent growth left Vancouver's old Chinatown with two distinct parts.

*Dr. Sun Yat-Sen Classical Chinese Garden is located near downtown Vancouver.*

Pender Street west of Main Street is quieter. Its historic nineteenth-century buildings display Asian touches such as recessed balconies and ornate wrought-iron railings. These buildings house organizations from earlier times that are still active because clan and home district loyalties remain important to some newcomers. New construction in this area bears witness to the post-1967 growth of the community. The Chinese Cultural Centre, its Museum and Archives building, and the Dr.

*Chinese going to fish near Burrard Inlet by Edward Roper, 1887.*

Sun Yat-sen Classical Garden have introduced more Chinese architecture, while the headquarters of SUCCESS and its long-term care facility are more pragmatic.

East of Main Street, along Pender and the streets south of it, Chinatown is a busy commercial district with stores, bakeries and restaurants. The streetscape has changed dramatically since the 1960s, as have the area's customers. Several recently built seniors' residences house the local patrons; others come from Strathcona, a thriving nearby residential area. The shops are glass, chrome and bright lights, reflecting recent infusions of immigrant capital and entrepreneurship.

## So Much Debt

In the 1880s the Chinese in the Vancouver area were employed at sawmills, dressing timber for export. After the CPR was built, the Chinese who came to Vancouver worked at the mills and cleared land. Racist whites chased them away twice. At the city's first election, one sawmill owner ran for mayor. He sent his Chinese workers to vote, but they were confronted by whites at the poll. A stagecoach driver whipped up four horses and chased them back to the mill.

The following year, when 20 Chinese were clearing land, 200 whites marched to their camp, razed the shacks and pushed the workers to the docks. From there, they were shipped to Victoria. When another Chinese crew arrived, whites raided the site again, burning bedding and clothing. The next morning, whites loaded Chinatown's residents onto wagons and sent them to New Westminster. But two weeks later they returned.

With the CPR ending at the harbour, where ships pushed trade further west and return traffic brought goods and immigrants from China, it was not surprising that Chinatown

*West coast fish canneries using Chinese crews, 1900.*

was near the docks, railway lines and the commercial downtown. Chinatown's first buildings were wood with flat false fronts. From the start, even though the city charter forbade non-whites from voting, Vancouver's Chinese merchants asserted the rights they did have and petitioned for improved sidewalks and other services in the 1890s.

Vancouver was near many canneries and served also as a centre for dispatching cannery workers to northern canneries. Canning was a complicated business, as one Chinese entrepreneur noted:

*I employ eight to one hundred hands; 20 per cent of them are white men. We have from fifty to sixty Chinese in the cannery. We employ fifteen to eighteen Indians inside the cannery. We had about twenty boats of white fisherman last year and from twelve to eighteen boats with Indians. The fishermen say there are too many boats. I think not too many boats, but too many canneries. White fisherman struck first last year. It was not easy to get fisherman to work for me last year. There was a lot of fish last year, but there was a strike on, and they did not go out and get them.*[1]

By 1907 four firms were earning annual incomes of $150,000 to $180,000. Chang Toy's Sam Kee Company had grown into a multi-armed enterprise. At age 17, Chang Toy had reached Victoria, his passage paid by a fish canner. But the boat had arrived late and only one month of work remained.

So Chang Toy worked for two years in a sawmill before starting a laundry in Vancouver. He then moved into import and export, retail, charcoal and fuel sales, labour contracting, steamship ticket sales and real estate. His firm had international links and traded extensively with white businesses. It sold rice to white wholesalers in Vancouver and approached similar firms in Calgary, Edmonton, Regina and Winnipeg. Between 1905 and 1915, its exports of salt herring to Asia tripled to 1540 tons. The Sam Kee Company also sent workers to harvest sugar beets in Alberta. It owned ten lots in Chinatown, and more land in the downtown and in surrounding municipalities.

Immigrants less fortunate than Chang Toy worked in Vancouver Chinatown's eight merchant-tailor firms or earned their living as clerks, cooks and porters for Chinese firms. A hundred Chinese farmers grew vegetables and raised pigs on farms.

As for laundries, the city restricted them to Chinatown. But by 1900, only two were still located there. The city then banned washing and drying clothes within sixty feet of any street. It called for compulsory smallpox vaccination of Chinese laundry workers and a ban on Sunday hours, and it required laundrymen to be listed as lodging-house keepers (so that they would come under housing bylaws). The Chinese hired lawyers to argue their case at City Hall, with the result that some but not all the bylaws were changed.

A laundryman with 18 years experience described his situation in 1902:

*I have hardly enough work to keep my men busy. I pay $20 a month rent. I am in debt now, because I have so much of debt that cannot be collected. … If I did not make so many bad debts I would earn something. … The largest amount of money that any man owes me for a bad debt is $100; one man owes me that. That man's washing comes to $5 a month. I have been washing for him since starting the laundry business. … Lots of them owe me from $10 to $20.*[2]

## Growing Pains

From 1901 to 1911, Vancouver's population quadrupled to 120,000 and its 3600 Chinese became Canada's largest such community. During this time, Chinese merchants erected brick buildings in Chinatown. But in September 1907, 8000 whites rampaged through Chinatown, hurling bricks and rocks to break every window and door. The riot, sparked by the Anti-Asiatic League, lasted five minutes but caused $3000 in damages and $20,000 of lost business. In protest, the Chinese went on strike for three days, abandoning hotels, restaurants, well-to-do homes, steamships and lumber mills. They purchased guns, and Chinatown's merchants hired watchmen to guard their property.

This hostility spurred immigrants to try to help modernize China. While Chinese Empire Reform Association (CERA) chapters spread across Canada, only in Vancouver did the association sponsor a school and a newspaper. The Chinese

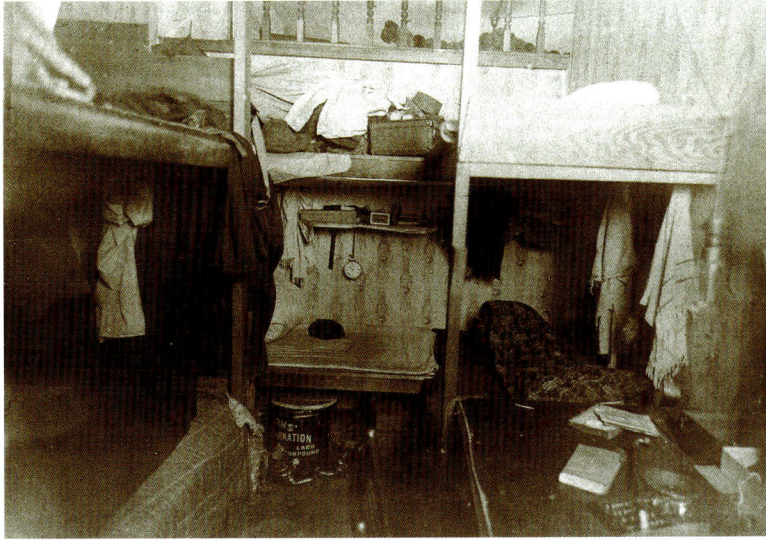

*Sleeping quarters for sixteen Chinese in a rooming house, 1902.*

Typical home of Vancouver white workingman

A Warren on Carrall Street infested by 2000 Chinese

*Cartoon from* Saturday Sunset *showing anti-Chinese racism, 1907.*

Freemasons also published a newspaper, the *Chinese Times*, in Vancouver. When Dr. Sun Yat-sen arrived in 1911, a thousand Chinese greeted him. For four days he spoke to huge audiences at Vancouver's Chinese Theatre. One participant recalled:

> *He spoke the same dialect I do, and so he spoke Cantonese with a Shek-Ki [Sek-kei] accent. Most people here were from Sze-yup [Sei-yup] and they didn't understand him. They said if Dr. Sun couldn't make them understand his speech, how was he going to get China back from the Manchus?*[3]

Clan and home district groups flourished. The Wongs, the Lees and the Chans were most numerous, as were migrants from Sei-yup. The Chinese Benevolent Association (CBA) ran a hospital and equipped a playground in Chinatown. And Christians taught English, along with the gospel.

## Boom and Bust

Like everyone on the Pacific coast, the Chinese faced boom-and-bust cycles in the economy. One recession began in 1912 after prairie demand for B.C. lumber dropped, leaving 80 percent of the city's Chinese jobless. Many returned to China,

*Artist Sing Lim depicted life in 1920s Chinatown.*

while residents faced destitution, food shortages and high prices. Other recessions occurred in 1916 and 1919.

In better times, the Chinese were farmers, grocers, peddlers and shingle makers. No job was easy. Farmers borrowed funds to lease land and buy seed. Grocers worked long hours and faced the spoilage of fresh produce. Peddlers' horses fell ill and clients didn't pay on time. Shingle mills involved dangerous saws and crude bunkhouses. One worker said:

*The mill had so many mosquitoes, you had to wrap up your face to work there. The sky would get dark, with so many mosquitoes! When you wanted to eat, you had to buy powder and light it before eating.*[4]

Some workers, notably shingle makers, formed unions. In July 1917 they went on strike with white co-workers, seeking shorter work hours. Since the Chinese formed 70 percent of the workforce, they briefly closed most factories in Vancouver and New Westminster. Two years later, when mill owners reduced workers' rates, the Chinese Shingle Workers Union called a strike that reinstated the original rates. Emboldened, the workers demanded payment for lost wages and won again.

Racism loomed over other work areas as well. White storekeepers demanded that the city regulate door-to-door peddlers. In 1918 a $100 licence fee was levied, but the lawyer for the Vegetable Sellers Association argued all the way to the Supreme Court that it was excessive. The association lost, but the fee was cut in half. Still, peddlers refused to pay because a store licence cost only $10. When angry peddlers went on strike, 5000 customers petitioned city hall for a fee reduction.

White storekeepers also fumed at Chinese grocers for "invading" white districts and working longer hours. The Retail Merchants Association, the local Board of Trade and local newspapers all called for a boycott of Chinese-run stores in 1922. They pushed for laws to limit the number of businesses that non-whites could own. The 1928 mayoral candidate said bluntly, "Oriental shops should be confined to fixed Oriental areas."

## A Different Kind of People

While the Chinese community was mostly male, women did come. Some were the wives of merchants, while others were sponsored to work as waitresses before being married to local men. There were 210 Chinese families in 1920, as Chinatown expanded into Strathcona, a residential district with a mix of

Japanese, Jews, Blacks and Eastern Europeans.

The Canadian-borns attended school but even they had difficulty finding jobs here. Some returned to China, but one fellow noted:

*China wanted people with experience. They didn't want to hire you. Before, everybody would say, 'Oh, you can always go back to China!' But the Chinese in China looked at the overseas Chinese as a different kind of people. I used to think the people over here were pretty smart. But I found out that the Chinese from China are pretty smart too.*[5]

Still, there were bright spots. In 1912 the city expropriated land owned by the Sam Kee Company. Instead of seizing the entire lot, the city left a worthless six-foot sliver of land. Undaunted, the company used the land to build the world's narrowest building. In 1921, Mrs. Nellie Yip, a white woman, Chinatown midwife and translator, successfully urged Vancouver's hospital to stop diverting Chinese patients to the hospital basement.

The Chinese soccer team won five major trophies in the 1920s and 1930s. *The Province* reported:

*They are always an entertaining team side to watch in action, as they play the game cleanly from start to finish. Moreover they are enthusiastic about the game and put everything they know into their play and their big asset on the field is the speed possessed by each member of the side. … They have been one of the biggest drawing cards in soccer in the city during the past year and whenever there was a call for charitable purposes they were among the first to respond.*

**Seeking Justice**

An unsolved murder highlighted racism in the justice system.

*Peter Lee of Kingston left his business card with the Yip Sang family of Vancouver, c1928.*

In 1924 Scottish nursemaid Janet Smith was found dead in a wealthy home. But, after an inquest ruled her death accidental, private detectives and policemen seized the houseboy Wong Foon Sing. They questioned and beat him. When a second inquest concluded Smith's death was not accidental, Wong mysteriously vanished. Six weeks later he was found, lost and dazed, having been severely beaten.

Wong said three men had seized him and blindfolded him. Two men dressed in white robes with hoods over their heads interrogated him. When he couldn't identify the murderer, they beat him. Over the weeks, the beatings worsened. At one point, a rope was put around his neck and strung over a beam. Amazingly, he was charged with Smith's murder.

*Cover of a silk firm catalogue, 1930s.*

Private detectives, police officers and members of Scottish groups were later charged with kidnapping Wong, but they were acquitted. Outraged, Vancouver's Chinese and the CBA rallied behind Wong, who was ultimately also acquitted.

Elsewhere, economic racism continued to be rampant. When Chinese greengrocers multiplied from 52 to 125 during 1925–35, and Chinese produce wholesalers rose from one in 1922 to 21 in fifteen years, alarmists feared that if the Chinese controlled the entire food industry, then whites would be at their mercy.

Meanwhile, new laws regulated the quantities and prices of farm produce allowed onto the market. Chinese farmers saw this as attempts to restrict their livelihood. When the farmers defied the marketing board by taking untagged potatoes to wholesalers in the 1930s, the "Potato Wars" erupted. The police barricaded bridges, but Chinese farmers drove their trucks through. When white farmers manned the barricades, tense and violent encounters resulted.

Café owners were also harassed. In 1935 police ordered three Chinatown café operators to dismiss their white waitresses, alleging that they were prostitutes for Chinese men. When the Licence Department threatened to withhold the cafés' business licences, angry waitresses told the mayor no work was available elsewhere. When they were fired, the women marched to city hall with the Vancouver Mothers' Council to protest.

During the Depression, 80 percent of Chinatown residents were idled in 1931, and some resorted to begging. By November, the CBA had exhausted its resources and turned to the city for help. The Chinese received less relief than whites, and destitute Chinese were dispatched to China because providing boat passage was cheaper than paying relief.

At the same time, Vancouver's Chinese embarked on 14 years

of intense fundraising to help China after Japan invaded in 1931. When World War II broke out, Ottawa refused to draft Chinese Canadians because British Columbia politicians feared they would claim the right to vote. Nevertheless, Chinese Canadians volunteered or enlisted in American forces before conscription was introduced in 1944.

After the war, the community lobbied against unfair immigration regulations. The chairman of Vancouver's CBA, Wong Foon Sien, travelled to Ottawa 11 times. He was outraged when a son born of a Chinese Canadian's second wife was refused entry. The Supreme Court of British Columbia, the British Columbia Court of Appeal and the Supreme Court of Canada all upheld the applicant's case, but Ottawa deftly passed a regulation forbidding such sponsorships. Eleven months after the Supreme Court's ruling, the applicant died. Wong Foon Sien wrote:

> Leong Hung Hing died … a bitter and heart-broken man, deprived of the privilege of having his son with him at his bedside in the last days of his life by, what to him at least, was an incomprehensible bureaucratic refusal … to follow the order and directions of the highest court of the land.
>
> I believe that most of the immigration officials have families. Their children on Christmas morning will sit on their fathers' knees and gleefully open parcels…
>
> I can not help but think about Leong Hung Hing's little boy who will certainly have no parcels to open on this day. He would not hear again words of encouragement from his … father whom he was unable to join and whom he will never see. He is wondering where his father is buried and will he permitted to come to gather some daisies to put on the grave in the spring and autumn as all dutiful sons should do.[6]

## Clash of Generations

In the 1950s the Vancouver Chinese community grew from 8700 to 15,000 as the wives and children of residents arrived. More sons came than daughters, because sponsoring fathers believed males could earn more money. On arrival, they attended classes for new Canadians or followed their fathers to work at lumber mills, ferries and restaurants. A few with English skills attended university; others were sent to small towns.

Not all went smoothly for these reunited families. Fathers who had lived frugally for decades balked at seeing their sons buy cars and tennis rackets. Their children were better educated, and Hong Kong had westernized them. Many sons were shocked at how plainly their fathers lived. Others wanted to return to help China's reconstruction. They formed new groups: the Chinese Youth Association openly supported Communist China, while the Hai Fung Club set up a library, gym and darkroom, and organized sports, speech contests and art exhibits.

Canadian-borns now began to move outside Chinatown. Charles Chan Kent's firm became Aero Garment Limited in 1952 and produced permanent press clothing. The H.Y. Louie Company acquired the IGA franchise for British Columbia in 1955. Individuals entered fields previously closed to them:

a man of *thought* *
a man of *action* *
a man of *achievement* *

**DOUG JUNG** *

**Centre's Conservative Candidate**

*First Chinese-Canadian Member of Parliament, 1957.*

*The famous neon signs of Pender Street, 1960s.*

the United Nations. Jung lost his seat in the 1962 election, but could have won if all the Chinese in the riding had voted for him. But their reluctance to vote on the basis of race was viewed as political maturity. They had voted on the issue, which in this case was a crackdown on illegal immigration.[7]

Old-timer Chinese and new immigrants continued to live in Chinatown and Strathcona. But the age of Chinatown's buildings and the stigma of being called "slums" put these areas at risk. In the 1960s blocks of Strathcona were bulldozed in attempts at "urban renewal." But residents fought back and started a self-help repair program for homes. As well, public protests stopped plans for freeways that would have destroyed Chinatown.

### Why Are People So Angry?

In the 1960s the old-timers were dying and the Canadian-born were joining the mainstream. It seemed Chinatown wasn't needed anymore.

In the 1970s, however, it was revitalized by an influx of immigrants from Hong Kong. New stores expanded the area's boundaries. Shops selling fashions, music and fresh foods multiplied, as did dim-sum houses, fast-food noodle outlets and bakery-cafés. The price of land skyrocketed and storefronts took on a sleek modern look. The city built a recreation centre for the growing community in Strathcona.

Some Hong Kong immigrants were prosperous, fluent in Chinese culture, and had English-educated children. But more were working-class families, arriving as sponsored relatives from the colony's resettlement estates (densely occupied, government-built apartment complexes) and Chinese-language schools. Some youngsters had difficulties based on language and class issues, which gave rise to "youth gangs" of disgruntled teens.[8]

pharmacy, law and chartered accountancy. Their children, a newly emerging third generation, grew up speaking little Chinese.

In the 1950s Chinatown briefly recovered from the decline started by the Great Depression. Several Chinese supermarkets and restaurants opened, Cantonese movies were screened, and furniture and appliance stores opened. New realty, insurance and finance companies sprang up, run by young entrepreneurs. By 1956 Chinatown boasted seven nightclubs, more than any other district, and attracted large numbers of whites. In the 1960s the restaurants boomed but the grocery stores declined.

In 1957 voters in the riding of Vancouver Centre elected war veteran Douglas Jung to the House of Commons, making him the first Chinese-Canadian Member of Parliament. Prime Minister Diefenbaker dispatched him to represent Canada at

Amid growing political confidence, both Canadian-born and immigrant Chinese won public office. New groups negotiated with the three levels of government over projects such as the Chinese Cultural Centre and the Dr. Sun Yat-sen Classical Gardens. The former opened its Phase One building in 1980, while the latter first welcomed visitors in 1986. The United Chinese Community Enrichment Services Society (SUCCESS) started in 1974 and evolved into a powerful social service agency and advocacy group.

Race relations in Vancouver improved: Chinese now lived everywhere, their festivals and events attracted non-Chinese, and school groups toured Chinatown. Canadian-born Chinese, in particular, had integrated into the mainstream through business, friendships and intermarriage. But reaction to the next wave of immigrants surprised many people.

Over 15 years, from 1986 to 2001, Vancouver took in 214,000 Chinese immigrants. They formed 45 percent of the newcomers to the city, coming from Hong Kong (101,000), China (57,000), and Taiwan (56,000). More Chinese immigrants went to Toronto, but Vancouver's smaller population made the growing Chinese presence more obvious.

In 1988 these newcomers were blamed for rising house prices. Between 1987 and 1989, the median house price on Vancouver's affluent west side jumped from $200,000 to $430,000. Longtime residents worried that their children wouldn't be able to afford a house, and the media singled out wealthy Hong Kong immigrants for increasing the demand and having the means to buy costly houses.

But the media ignored other factors. Offshore investors in Asia, as well as elsewhere in the world, were also keen to invest in Vancouver. Net migration from other provinces to Vancouver was 38,000 in the 1987–89 period, more than double the 16,000 immigrants from Hong Kong, China and Taiwan. And a shortage of housing reflected natural demography: baby-boomers had reached home-buying age.[9]

Chinese immigrants were also vilified for building oversize houses and cutting down mature trees. In fact, their houses had been built within zoning bylaws; it was builders and contractors who had assumed Chinese buyers wanted big houses and minimal landscaping. Although the city amended home construction bylaws several times, feelings grew bitter, and construction sites were often vandalized.

Other resentments surfaced in the media. People ranted about newcomers being poor car drivers and rude shoppers,

*Section of the Dr. Sun Yat-Sen Classical Chinese Garden.*

while parents complained that immigrant children flaunted their wealth and refused to speak English. Long-arrived Chinese immigrants were quoted when they criticized the newcomers. This strengthened anti-immigrant sentiment by implying that if Chinese people disapproved of their own kind, then white people who felt the same way should not be labelled racist.

> Why are people in Vancouver so angry?" asked S.Y. Lee, a Hong Kong broker. "Your government really wanted investment money to generate the economy, so it opened the door to investors. The mayor of your city, your premier, they all came to Hong Kong to invite people to Vancouver. … How would you feel if someone invited you to their home and then when you showed up, they say, 'You're not welcome'?[10]

Another battleground involved schools again. By 1988 half of Vancouver's 50,000 students did not have English as their mother tongue, so the costs of English-as-a-Second-Language (ESL) classes rose. Longtime residents grumbled about their children not getting the courses they wanted and valuable class time being lost to students with English problems. In Vancouver and adjacent Richmond, newcomer students were surrounded by fellow immigrants, which slowed the learning of English. Some immigrant parents moved to distant suburbs in order to help their children.

Other Chinese parents said Canadian schools were academically weak and lax on discipline. In 1998 they asked the Vancouver School Board for a publicly funded traditional school that would emphasize discipline, a back-to-basics curriculum, uniforms and more homework. After much public debate, the request was rejected.

Similar issues arose in Richmond, where by 2000 almost 40 percent of the population was Chinese, the highest concentration in Canada. Immigrants liked the low house prices, the convenience of Chinese retailers, and the closeness of the airport. Large Chinese malls emerged, but, with their lack of English-language signage, helpful staff and North American food, they were labeled "unfriendly."

Race relations deteriorated amidst reports of white residents moving away because the English-speaking population was declining. When parents of Chinese students formed a group, the existing parents worried about segregation. When residents of a mostly Chinese street objected to a proposed drug-recovery home on their street, the not-in-my-back-yard debate became racially charged. And one parent launched a heated debate in the local newspaper, objecting to Richmond employers wanting Chinese-speaking staff. Letter writers accused each other of being racist, while others condemned using the label "racist" to silence the expression of community opinions.[11] With the passing of time, these tensions gradually waned.

## Ghost Town

Ironically, immigration brought bad news for Vancouver's old Chinatown. At first, newcomers had boosted property values, investments and sales. Then business slowed as Chinese products became available in suburban supermarkets and malls. Groups like the Chinese Cultural Centre, SUCCESS and the Taiwanese Canadian Cultural Society all opened satellite operations in the suburbs.

Chinatown's designation as a "heritage" district blocked new uses and renovations to buildings located in its historic section, west of Main Street. Incidents of break-ins, shoplifting and street mugging increased and were blamed on the transient, low-income residents of the adjoining Downtown Eastside and on the drug trade.

Throughout the 1990s improvements occurred within the

heritage designation. New buildings went up: a mall with lots of parking and a vast Chinese restaurant, banking facilities, residential projects, the headquarters of SUCCESS, and a 100-bed intermediate-care facility. The Chinatown Merchants Association sponsored open-air "night markets" for several summers. With the opening of nearby GM Place, it was hoped people would park cheaply in Chinatown, stroll to GM Place, and then return to Chinatown for a meal.

But by 1999 all the neon signs along Pender Street were gone as diners abandoned Chinatown and restaurants closed. The best Chinese food was now found in suburban neighbourhoods. "Chinatown used to be the place to go at night," said one businessman. "Nowadays, after 6 o'clock, it's like a ghost town."[12]

*Outdoor mural celebrating old Chinatown as a historic site, 1990s.*

Chinatown east of Main Street remained busy as crowds and stores spread south. In 2001 the three levels of government funded the Chinatown Millennium Gate, hoping to reinvigorate the western edge of the district with a traditional Chinese archway. As well, the Chinatown Revitalization Committee was formed to create a vision for the future.

## Sensitive Issues

After the Tiananmen Square incident of June 1989, most of Vancouver's Chinese denounced the bloodshed. But China's unrepentant defence of its crackdown forced local groups to review their positions. For example, when the Dr. Sun Yat-sen Classical Gardens' board rejected a statue of the Goddess of Democracy for the garden, the board was accused of siding with China. Or, when democracy supporters proposed a commemorative plaque for a Vancouver park, the CBA denounced it as "blatant interference with the internal affairs of another country."

Another divisive issue was the question of "head tax redress." Some Chinese began seeking a refund from Ottawa of entry taxes paid by early immigrants under the pre-1947 exclusion laws. Old-timers in Vancouver started the issue and then Toronto's Chinese Canadian National Council adopted it. New immigrants pursued redress (including an apology from the government) on the principle that the taxes had undermined the human rights and dignity of the Chinese. Chinese Canadians did not unanimously support redress. The claim failed in 1994, but supporters pushed it onto the stage of the United Nations.

Newcomers also resented certain media coverage. In March 1989 callers to Chinese-language radio complained for three hours about how the media's obsession with wealthy immigrants ignored the middle-class majority. In 1991, after CBC-Radio broadcast "Dim Sum Diaries," a play about immigrant Chinese issues, a petition accused the CBC of provoking racial violence and reinforcing hatred of the Chinese. Other people were less reactive. A Hong Kong journalist asked, "Is it racism or over-defensiveness?" and reminded people that plays were not documentary reports and allowed for exaggeration.[13]

Hong Kong newcomers were at the centre of other issues as well. "Astronaut" immigrants were accused of avoiding taxes and not committing to life in Canada. It didn't help matters when they complained about the slow pace of business in Canada. The tax issue was more insidious because no proof existed. Anyone with a family or home in Canada was required to report his or her worldwide income. But without a tax treaty with Hong Kong or Taiwan, Canada could not verify earnings abroad. When 1995 government legislation required all Canadians to report their foreign assets, immigrants from Hong Kong and Taiwan opposed it, and also blamed it for Asia-bound return migration.

**Art Is Important**

The world of the arts has proved to be a bridge between cultures. Vancouver's Chinese attended "mainstream" art events, and also appreciated Asian TV series, movies, literature and music. They also generated talent. Amateur groups practised traditional Chinese music and opera. Musicians "crossed over": Lan Tung of Orchid Ensemble improvised at the 1999 Vancouver International Jazz Festival, and Vivienne Wang's opera "Peach Project" was sung in both Taiwanese and English. Asian artists in the B.C. Chamber Orchestra and B.C. Sinfonietta performed Western and Chinese classics, and the Kiwanis Festival began to feature a category for Chinese Ethnic Instruments.

Other artists portrayed immigrant experiences. Lorita Leung premiered Gold Mountain in 2000, and then composers and dancers mounted "Gold and Maple Dreams", another dance creation. Chinese-language writers produced newsletters, magazines and anthologies. Other writers worked in English, and investigated history. SKY Lee portrayed several generations of one family, while Wayson Choy and Denise Chong explored childhoods in the 1940s. From the diaspora came authors such as Goh Poh Seng from Malaysia, Thuong Vuong-Riddick from Vietnam and Laiwan from Zimbabwe.

Issues of personal and family identity emerged on stage from playwright Betty Quan and on screen from filmmakers Karin Lee, Colleen Leung and Mina Shum. These issues also sparked art exhibitions such as "Self Not Whole" (which included longtime local artists Paul Wong and Sharyn Yuen) and multimedia programs such as "Racy Sexy."

The anti-immigrant backlash of the late 1980s and early 1990s had surprised Vancouver, given its long history of Chinese settlement. What happened? In the past, immigrants had been landless peasants and the urban poor who worked up from the bottom, toiling at menial jobs. They accepted a loss of dignity as the price of entry and never challenged the privileges of the middle and upper classes.

In earlier times, Asia's educated middle classes had enjoyed high status at home. Then, politics in the 1980s and 1990s sent them to Canada in large numbers. They came expecting equal treatment. After all, hadn't Canada's Citizenship Act of 1947 declared Canadian-born and foreign-born to be equal? As such, the new immigrants challenged Canadians in a way that pre-1923 immigrants did not.

*A Chinatown landmark, housing long-time newspaper and musical group, 1993.*

# 3

# CALGARY: COWTOWN CHINATOWN

One striking aspect of Calgary's skyline is a large, volcano-shaped roof, with slopes of blue glazed tile and a golden orb at the top. Although dwarfed by nearby skyscrapers, this roof floats over Calgary's Chinese Cultural Centre and attracts many visitors. Inside, the ceiling features a spiral dragon, and gold-leaf lotus patterns adorn the columns. A team of 22 artisans from China used traditional tools and techniques to finish the roof in 1992, modelling it after that of

*Directors of Calgary's Chinese Cultural Centre on roof, 1992.*

the Hall of Prayers in Beijing's Imperial Palace complex.

Calgary's Chinatown has survived at its old location by the Bow River, but it is now dominated by new shopping malls and several residential towers for seniors. The single-family houses from earlier days have all disappeared. Chinatown's northern boundary is Sien Lok Park, which proudly shows Chinese and Chinese-Canadian influences: the yin-yang circle embedded into the courtyard, the formal gazebo, and two monuments ("In Search of Gold Mountain" and "Wall of Names") honouring Chinese-Canadian pioneers. The park's main sponsor, the Sien Lok Society, continues to be very active in community affairs.

### A Festering Sore

When the first Chinese reached Calgary, Edmonton and Lethbridge, they started cafés and laundries and also grew vegetables that they sold from door to door. In smaller Albertan towns, they ran cafés and laundries. Others worked in sugar factories or mined for coal around Bankhead or Canmore.

After the completion of the CPR in 1885, unemployed Chinese railway workers came to Calgary, then a North West Mounted Police fort. The first Chinese laundries opened northeast of the railway station, and the area around Eighth and Ninth Avenues SW at Third Street SE became the first Chinatown, with eight eateries, one tailor, one grocer and several laundries.

Few archival details survive from these early years but one incident stands out. In June 1892 a Chinese just returned from Vancouver fell ill with smallpox. City officials burned the laundry where he lived. They quarantined four Chinese outside town, and put them under North West Mounted Police guard. Still, nine people contracted the disease and three died.

Two months later, the four Chinese released from quarantine returned to Chinatown. That night, a mob of 300 men attacked the laundries, smashing doors and windows, trying to start fires and chase the Chinese out of town. A few Chinese were badly injured, but most fled, some to the Mounted Police barracks and others to the homes of church officials. It took several hours to disband the mob, and the Mounted Police patrolled the city for three weeks to prevent further violence.

*Chinese section men on Canadian Pacific Railway handcars, c1886.*

A second Chinatown emerged on the other side of the railway tracks. By 1900 there were 63 Chinese in Calgary. They wanted to learn English at Knox Presbyterian Church, but congregation members objected. Thomas Underwood, a Baptist, a builder and later a mayor of Calgary, who had known the Chinese during railway construction, generously erected a two-room building for the Chinese on his land at First Street SW near Tenth Avenue SW.

When that building became too small, Underwood built a larger Chinese Mission there and the second Chinatown sprang up around it. Its "shacks" were densely populated:

*Almost every room in the building held Chinese men, talking, gambling, smoking and sleeping. The building is partitioned off in narrow sections and these sections are*

*Students and teachers at the Chinese Mission, 1902.*

*again partitioned off in [infinitesimal] rooms. The building has three floors, the ground floor, a first floor and a basement. Every inch of these parts is utilized.*[1]

This Chinatown did not last. During the first decade of the new century, white settlers flooded into the prairies, and Calgary's population tripled to 44,000. The city's economy relied on beef and agriculture, industries subject to uncertain prices, drought and boom-bust cycles. During one such boom, the CNR decided to build a depot downtown, causing land values near the second Chinatown to soar. Since the Chinese had only rented homes and businesses, they were evicted. By the decade's end, only 500 Chinese still lived in Calgary.

Their merchants then purchased land at Centre Street at Second Avenue SE. But nearby property owners objected, supported by the city's top newspaper. The *Calgary Herald* said:

*If the Chinese build a block at Second Avenue and Centre Street, it naturally follows that property all along there will be depreciating in value. White people will be glad to sell out and Chinese will be glad to buy at cheap prices. Thus like a festering sore their presence will spread from block to block to their own profit and the city's detriment.*[2]

Merchant Louie Kheong wrote back, deftly criticizing Western hypocrisy:

*I take your paper and see that some people in Calgary are saying some bad things about my countrymen here. This is not right. The Canadian government has given us the right to live here and pay our debts. We want to do honest business in Calgary same as all men and Canada's law will protect us. You send missionaries to our homes in China, and we use them good; also English business men. If my people are no good to live here, what good trying to make them go to Heaven? Perhaps there will only be my people there.*[3]

City officials, such as the medical health officer, sided with the Chinese, however. Mackie, the chief of police, noted that the Chinese were law-abiding and not troublesome,[4] and the city let the third Chinatown proceed.

Chiefs who followed Mackie were less tolerant, sharing the popular view that Chinatown contained unsavoury and criminal elements. In the 1910 decade, except during the war years, the police raided Chinatown repeatedly. They crashed through doors to charge suspects with illegal gambling and opium use. Many of the arrested men hired white lawyers to defend them in court. In 1914 Calgary's Chinese sued the police chief and the city for unlawful entry, and fought the case all the way to the Supreme Court of Canada before being defeated.

Cattle ranching was important to southern Alberta, and Calgary's early Chinese had two connections to it. Many cattle ranchers hired Chinese chefs, who not only cooked and baked but also tended chickens and raised vegetables for the meals. As well, they washed the cowboys' laundry and did barn chores. Hired in the spring before haying, they stayed until after the fall round-up. Then they went to Calgary to pass the winter.[5]

The other tie to the cattle industry occurred later and involved Ho Lem, who arrived in Calgary in 1901. When he opened the Belmont Café several years later, he learned that the local stockyards were throwing out tons of calf livers because no one wanted them. Ho Lem took the liver and developed a liver and onions dish that became popular with the cowboys and workers who were his customers. Ho Lem's success eventually led the stockyards to put a price on the livers.[6]

**New Community Leaders**

The new century began the Canadian-born generation in Calgary. The first Chinese woman arrived in 1905, and a year later, the city recorded its first Chinese birth.

Louie Kheong had arrived in Calgary in 1894 and set up the first Chinese store. His compatriot Ho Lem came in 1901, after working in Vancouver. Once in Calgary, it took six months for him to land a dishwashing job paying $10 a month. But he soon became a cook and opened his own café five years later. In 1917 Ho Lem expanded his business range: his Calgary Knitting Company imported equipment and wool from England to produce sweaters and ladies' suits. He was the first Chinese to join the Canadian Manufacturers Association as well as the Calgary Chamber of Commerce. While the mill provided jobs to local Chinese, the garment industry proved tough. So Ho Lem signed on with Sun Life Assurance, travelling throughout Alberta to sell insurance policies to Chinese.

*Above: Chinese leaders discussed the third Chinatown with city officials, 1910.*
*Below: Ho Lem, prominent entrepreneur, 1940.*

Calgary kept growing until World War I, and the tally of Chinese-run grocery stores, restaurants and laundries rose to 100 in 1915. Buck Doo Yee came to Canada in 1914 at the age of 25 and worked for over 60 years in a laundry. In a 1974 interview, he recalled the hardships of his early working life:

*I came to Calgary by train. At first, I lived with friends and relatives, about ten of us living together. At that time, people were very poor and the restaurant*

*sold them to us only a few cents for many pounds. Later I worked in a laundry. There was no hot water, so I had to boil some water to wash the clothes. Everything was done with my bare hands, therefore my hands were full of blisters and bleeding all the time by contacting too much soap and washing soda.*[7]

As the number of Chinese increased, they formed surname groups to help members with jobs, housing and other essentials. The Louie, Fong and Kwong groups were organized in 1915, the Wongs in 1918, the Mahs in 1918, the Yees in 1919 and the Leongs in 1923.

China's politics also reached Calgary. By 1910, 200 people belonged to the Chinese Empire Reform Association branch that Louie Kheong presided over. After Dr. Sun Yat-sen visited Calgary in March of 1911, a branch of the Chinese Freemasons was formed. His supporters in Calgary raised more than $3000.[8] Two years after the revolution's success, the Calgary branch of the Kuomingtang (KMT), Dr. Sun's party in China, was formed.

Thereafter, political troubles in China prompted Calgary KMT members to respond. When a northern warlord tried to become emperor in 1916, Chinese headed for China to join the army. In 1922, when a renegade general drove Dr. Sun from the presidential palace, Calgary KMT members raised funds for guns to protect him. Amidst such patriotism, it was not surprising that the KMT became Calgary's largest Chinese group, with 450 members in 1923.

The rivalry between the Freemasons and the KMT continued. In 1918 two Freemasons were convicted of attempted murder after attacking two KMT members with knives and bars in an alley. A few months later, some Freemasons beat two KMT men senseless. The ensuing charges and counter-charges occupied the courts for some time.

*Chinese YMCA hockey team included Frank Ho Lem, back left.*

*business was not good so sometimes we didn't get paid. We had to grow some vegetables and potatoes at the back yard. We had to eat beef livers and pork livers. One day, a white woman saw that we were eating livers, thus she*

### "China, Christ, Canada"

A key group in the community was the Chinese Mission, a non-denominational church. Early members such as Luey Dofoo, Louie Kheong, Luey Chow and Ho Lem had learned English there and gone on to become local leaders. In 1912 the Chinese Mission set up Calgary's "Chinese YMCA," the first YMCA of its kind in Canada. It became a popular spot, with 275 men in its recreation and education programs.

By 1920 some 39 Chinese children lived in the city, and a Chinese Public School provided language training. This Canadian-born generation was small, as Calgary still had only 15 Chinese families. At the Chinese Mission, they formed the David Yui Hi-Y hockey team in 1928, and a girls' basketball team, Jun Gon (True Light), the following year. In 1932 they started the Chinese Young People's Society and published a monthly magazine, the CCC ("China, Christ, Canada"). David Ho Lem led the six-member Chinese Hawaiian Orchestra, which included his brothers George and Ernie, George Lem, Si Dofoo and Jack Kheong. The mission's basketball team won the Church League Championship in 1948.

The Canadian-born also faced racial discrimination. Normie Kwong, born in Calgary in 1929, recalled:

> "When I was a boy, there was a park at the top of the Centre Street hill. I used to always want to go wading in the pool there, but I wasn't allowed because it was just for white people. There was no sign or anything; it's just the way things were."[9]

The Depression brought misery to many, but the Chinese were particularly affected. By the 1930s, 1000 Chinese resided in Calgary. Fifty jobless Chinese found shelter at the Chinese Mission, where its Mothers' Club helped feed them. There the men formed the Unemployed Men's Choir.

*Girls dressed for a special event at the Chinese Mission, 1934.*

Each single jobless Chinese received $1.12 per week in provincial relief, while a white applicant got $2.50. The Chinese protested against this racist treatment, but to no avail. In 1936 the province cut payments to 48 Chinese when they refused to go to a relief camp. Led by the Communist Party of Canada, the Chinese picketed government offices and massed at Calgary City Hall to demand civic relief. Police were called to disperse them. During other protests, Chinese were arrested.

In January 1937, 80 Chinese protested the unfair relief rates by holding the first of several sit-downs on the city's streetcar tracks. In February the police arrested thirteen Chinese at one such protest. Eventually, the government did raise the rates for the Chinese to $2.12 per week.

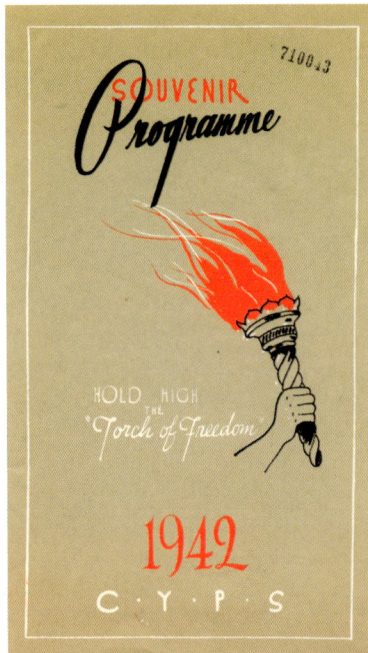

In March, the city learned that three Calgary Chinese had recently died of malnutrition. When the health officer inspected Chinatown, he shut down several buildings because of health issues. But, as no alternative housing was offered, the 28 destitute Chinese who were evicted ended up at the Chinese Mission, sleeping on the floor.

During the Sino-Japanese War and World War II, white Canadians admired Chinese fundraising efforts and saw Chinese Canadians enlist. In 1937 Alberta's Chinese set up the Pan Alberta Anti-Japanese League in Calgary, with branches in Edmonton, High River, and Medicine Hat. Calgary's Chinese raised over $200,000 for China's war effort between 1937 and 1945.[10]

Although pioneer Louie Kheong died in Calgary in 1939, his family had travelled back to China some years earlier. There, his sons Harry, Joe, Jack and Ken joined the Chinese and American armed forces. Two brothers from the Dofoo family also went to China in 1941 to work.

Back home, many young Chinese joined the Canadian military. Ho Lem's eldest son, Frank, had been a sergeant in the Canadian Reserve Army. In 1939 he signed up, and went on to serve at the Currie Barracks as a small arms instructor and become the first Chinese-Canadian Commissioned Officer. Thirty other Chinese Calgarians enlisted for service. Diamond Quon of the Royal Canadian Corps of Signals served in Italy and Belgium. He was killed in action on March 12 1945 at the age of 23.[11]

**After the War**

The post–World War II years saw renewed growth among the Chinese. After 1947 the number of Chinese in Calgary rose to 973 in 1951, and then to 2232 in 1961. With changes in the immigration laws, the wives and offspring of the old-timers arrived from China. Other Alberta Chinese also came to work in Calgary's oil industry and to raise families. In 1956 the Chinese Public School reopened for a new crop of Canadian-born children.

The Canadian-born now enjoyed a high profile: Normie Kwong played professional football with the Calgary

*Above: Souvenir programme for wartime fundraising, 1942.*
*Below: Church choir that toured Alberta for wartime fundraising, 1940.*

Stampeders, Jennie Chow was crowned Queen of the Calgary Stampede in 1958, and in 1959 George Ho Lem was the first Chinese elected to a Canadian city council. Chinese Canadians were seen as valuable members of society as they joined the Community Chest drive, sponsored a prize-winning float in the Alberta Golden Jubilee parade in 1955, and formed clubs for curling, bowling and golf.

Growth at that time arose mostly from family reunification. One 1949 arrival was Roddy Mah, whose father owned a Centre Street restaurant. Although Mah had been born in Calgary in 1929, he had been sent to China when he was five. When he returned at the age of 20, he spoke no English, a situation shared by fellow immigrants. These young people had to learn English and find work quickly. Mah started high school at Mount Royal College, and worked at his father's restaurant and at a grocery store. Eventually, he became a partner in a café, and then he and his wife opened a restaurant.

A woman who arrived in 1950 recalled thinking that Calgary's Chinese were half a century behind the new Chinese immigrants due to their traditional behaviour. During that decade, about 250 young mail-order brides came to Calgary from Hong Kong. The only information they had about their future husbands came from the go-betweens. These women worked long hours or helped in family businesses, and found little time for recreation.[12]

**A Well to Return to**

As public opinions about Chinese Canadians improved, people wondered if Chinatowns were still needed. During the years of declining numbers, Calgary's Chinatown had become dilapidated, making it an easy target for demolition. But a new phase started as the community grew larger and more confident. Members began to view Chinatown as a symbol of

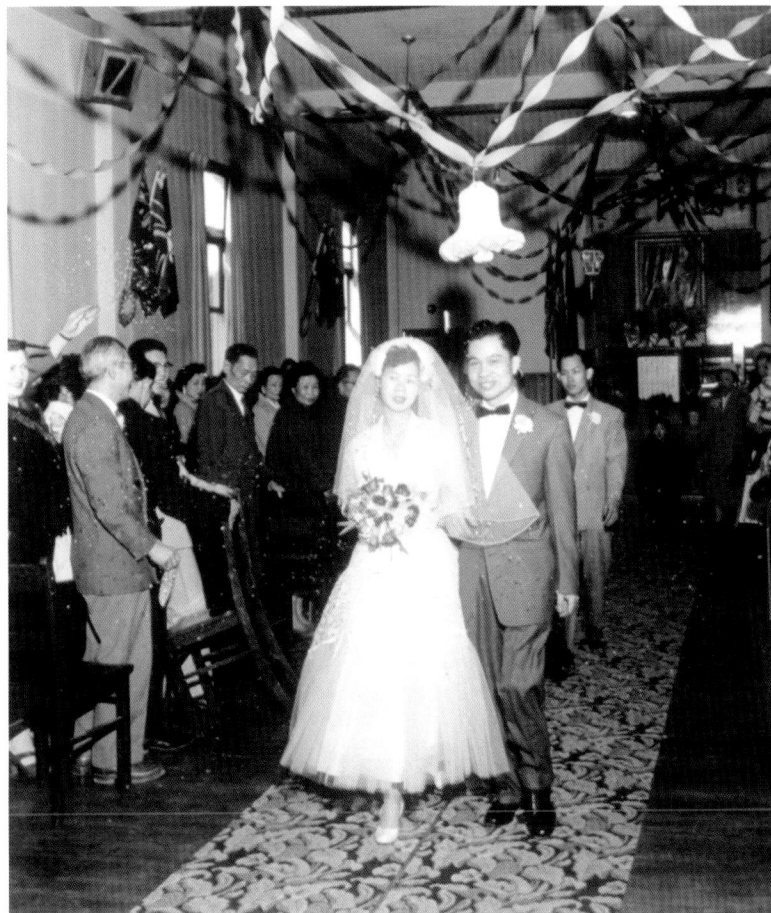

*Mail-order bride Shin Gam Len from Hong Kong married Geem Sam Yuen, 1957.*

their history in the city and their ongoing visibility as a racial minority.

In the 1960s, although the numbers of Chinese residents kept increasing, almost doubling to 4630 in 1971, these newcomers did not choose to live in Chinatown, and its population fell. By

*Above: 1966 view of the school before its demolition in 1977.*
*Below: 1967 view of Centre Street, threatened by urban renewal.*

1971, of 811 people living there, only 492 were Chinese. No wonder that in 1966 the city proposed the Bow Trail Extension, a 12-lane freeway that would swallow half of Chinatown. A new Centre Street Bridge would also carve into Chinatown.

The Chinese were told to build a new Chinatown elsewhere. At first, the end of Chinatown seemed inevitable. Some businessmen did not think much of the idea to relocate Chinatown but felt that progress was inevitable and a move might even improve the look of the community.[13]

Then a movement arose to save Chinatown. In 1968 Canadian-born Chinese professionals and businesspeople formed the Sien Lok Society. They complained that the city had not consulted the Chinese community about Chinatown's future. The society drew national attention when it organized a 1969 conference on the effects of urban renewal on Canadian Chinatowns. At the conference, Ray Lee, the president of Sien Lok, said, "To the Chinese Canadians like myself who do not reside in the core, we look to Chinatown as a social-psychological well to which we can return to refresh ourselves."[14]

Sien Lok later joined the United Calgary Chinese Association (UCCA), an umbrella group containing the older organizations of Chinatown. Despite this apparent solidarity, however, Chinatown still declined. In 1973 the construction of a federal government complex between First and Second Streets SE caused many bungalows to be bulldozed and 200 residents were relocated. The Bow Trail Extension project was revived in 1973. Only after Chinese community protests did the city set up a task force to draft an area plan. The resulting design called for non-profit housing for low-income people and senior citizens, and suggested sites for housing, community facilities and mixed development. City Council approved the plan in 1976.

That year marked a turning point as the first Chinese United Church seniors' towers opened. The Lee Family

Association, the Chinese Public School and the Calgary Chinatown Development Foundation built Bowside Manor, with 88 units of non-profit housing and space for the language school. Another family group, the Mahs, built a five-storey apartment and retail complex in 1978. When the Chinese United Church's second seniors' tower opened, 200 applicants vied for 126 spaces.

By this time, Chinatown's potential had become apparent thanks to its proximity to Calgary's central business district. When a businessman tried to convert low-rent apartments in Chinatown into upscale suites for business travellers, the UCCA bitterly opposed him. Chinatown's economy had improved as Calgary's Chinese population grew during the 1970s, reaching 16,000 in 1981 as a result of immigration from Hong Kong.

As the economic stakes in Chinatown's growth intensified, contending visions for Chinatown arose among district landowners in 1982. The newly formed Calgary Ratepayers' Association advocated high-density office, commercial and housing construction, while the UCCA wanted smaller buildings and more residential apartments. Each side claimed it had the community's backing. The battle stalled until a compromise two years later allowed medium to high density construction in the heart of Chinatown, and higher density commercial use at its perimeter. As a trade-off, landowners who won extra development rights vowed to help fund the Chinese Cultural Centre.

As immigration from Hong Kong rose further in the late 1980s, land values in Chinatown soared for a while. Dragon City opened in 1994 as Canada's largest Chinese mall. Then, the recession of the early 1990s caused businesspeople to look towards a casino proposal to improve Chinatown's economy. But many Chinese Canadians opposed the plan, and City Council

eventually blocked such developments in Chinatown.

In the late 1990s Calgary's Chinatown became key to the city's new vision of a repopulated downtown core containing viable residential districts. Upscale condominium projects went up nearby. Some people called Chinatown "the liveliest place in the downtown." Indeed, its commercial success had pushed it north, across the river, to establish businesses along Centre Street North.

*Above: Chinatown construction boom, 1990.*
*Below: Chinatown, 2004.*

*Dragon City Mall, touted as Canada's largest Asian mall when it was built, 2004 view.*

## Calgary Is Very Friendly

In the new millennium, Calgary's Chinese represented diverse backgrounds. For example, as the community strove to raise $8 million to build Calgary's Chinese Cultural Centre in the late 1980s, organizers recognized the predominance of Hong Kong immigrants and brought in high-profile entertainers Roman Tam, Leslie Cheung, Patrick Tse and Anita Mui. Smaller fundraising events were linked to mainstream events such as the Calgary Stampede and the Winter Olympics.

Calgary had attracted many Hong Kong immigrants in the late 1980s. Stock trader Roger Lam arrived in 1989 after seeing the city's modern look and efficient roads. "Toronto was too busy, while Vancouver seemed too quiet—too many retired people," he said. A banker praised other features: "Calgary is very friendly, the crime rate is low, and you can bring in half a million to buy a house and car and still have $250,000 left to invest," she said.[15]

An estimated 130 Hong Kong entrepreneurs established or invested in firms creating 400 full-time jobs in the city between 1996 and 1999. Not all Hong Kong immigrants were wealthy, however, and some skilled professionals couldn't find work. One said, "They [employers] think we are all quite wealthy, and won't be serious about our job."[16]

After 1994 Hong Kong immigration fell behind that from mainland China. At the same time, Calgary saw opportunities in China for developing housing, setting up joint ventures, and selling high tech. Firms such as Fracmaster Limited, Husky Oil and Sunwing Energy responded to China's need for foreign oil producers. Advance Drilling Limited had two drilling rigs built in China and shipped to Canada because it couldn't get rigs locally during the boom.[17] Fittingly, Calgary was twinned with the city of Daqing, in the heart of China's oil region.

When China established a consulate in Calgary in 1998, political issues were highlighted. When Nobel Prize nominee Wei Jingsheng (a labour and democracy advocate in China) spoke in Calgary in 1998, local organizers accused the consulate of interfering with room bookings. Then, when the mayor refused to present Wei with the city's traditional white cowboy hat, Wei's supporters demanded an apology. After the 1999 Taiwan earthquake, Calgary's Taiwanese rallied for a protest at the consulate, accusing China of blocking their attempts to send aid. And China's National Day celebrations invited protests by groups such as the Movement for Democracy in China and the Canada Tibet Committee.

Chinatown's traditional organizations remained active as new immigrants joined them. In 1999 Calgary's Toy San Association built a concrete and granite memorial on the MacLeod Trail near

Cemetery Hill to commemorate the city's early Chinese settlers. The memorial marked the reburial of 39 bodies removed from the Chinese Cemetery during construction of the Light Rapid Transit. One organizer said, "We believe that these pioneers deserve better treatment and they should be properly honoured so that they can rest in peace."[18]

### A Lot More to Offer

By the twenty-first century, Calgary's Chinese communities were fourth-largest in Canada, forming at least 5 percent of the city's population and its largest visible minority. Local people claimed there were 80,000 Chinese, rather than the census count of 52,000. Of that, a third were Canadian-born; of the immigrants, almost half had arrived after 1991.

The Chinese communities flourished. They enjoyed radio broadcasts in Chinese as well as Chinese pay-TV. The Board of Education started a Mandarin bilingual program in 1998, and during 1981–87, enrolment at the Chinese Public School quadrupled to 800 as immigrants and Canadian-born Chinese wanted to be sure that their offspring learned about their heritage. This concern was partly addressed when dragon boat races started in 1992. Forty-five thousand people attended the 1993 event at North Glenmore Park and cheered on 60 teams from across North America.

The Calgary Chinese communities resisted being seen as inward-looking. The Chinese Cultural Centre (CCC) opened in September 1992. Seven years later, Victor Mah, its chairman since the start, said:

> At the time it was built ... I said the completion of the building is the first step; success depends on how people will use it. I'm very happy about the outcome. It is really multicultural now. Our community happens to be part of downtown. We feel we have a lot more to offer to the entire city and province than just being a small ethnic community.[19]

The activities of the CCC have included non-Chinese events such as political meetings, citizenship ceremonies, concerts of the Calgary Philharmonic Orchestra, and art exhibits of local and international work.

At the same time, the past has remained a part of Calgary's Chinese present. In 1998 Globe and Mail columnist Jan Wong addressed a luncheon audience in Calgary at the invitation of the city's Famous Five Foundation, which was erecting statues of the five Alberta women who won legal recognition as "persons" in 1929. Wong set the historical record straight by reading from a 1922 book written by one of the Famous Five, who accused Chinese people of planning "the downfall of the white race" with opium.

As Wong recalled, "The audience was completely silent. I didn't know if they were going to boo or throw things."

She received a standing ovation.[20]

*Cantonese opera performance at Chinatown festival, 2001.*

# 4

# WINNIPEG: GATEWAY TO THE WEST...OR EAST?

When talking about Winnipeg's Chinatown, people are careful. As one writer wrote of it: 'Everything has beauty, but not everyone sees it.'[1]

Chinatown in Winnipeg is downtown, between North Main in the city's oldest neighbourhood, and the Exchange in the business core. These areas have both benefited from massive public funding for urban redevelopment. City Hall is close to Chinatown, but so is Main Street's skid row.

A Chinese gate spans King

*Winnipeg Chinese Cultural and Community Services Centre, 2004.*

Street and doubles as a covered sky-walk. On one side are the Dynasty Building, with two tiers of eastern-styled roofs, the Chinese Cultural and Community Services Centre (CCCSC), and a garden of ponds and ornamental rock. On the other side, the Mandarin Building holds two grand statues of Chinese gods.

However, the rest of Chinatown is rather run down, containing deserted buildings and empty lots. There have been calls for Chinese businesses to locate in Chinatown rather than elsewhere. There is little housing for a residential base. On weekdays the streets are quiet but they grow busy on the weekends, when customers from rural Manitoba, Kenora or Thompson, for example, come to stock up.

**Everybody Washed and Ironed**

The early Chinese in Winnipeg saw two differences from other western cities. When they reached central Canada, cities there were already thriving. In contrast, on the Pacific coast they had seen first-hand the births of Victoria and Vancouver, and could claim to be city pioneers. When the Chinese reached Winnipeg in November 1877, the city's 2000 residents had already built a city hall. Notably, Charley Yam, Fung Quong and a Chinese woman had not travelled eastward from the Pacific Ocean and through the Rocky Mountains. Rather, they had taken a stagecoach north from the United States, where one of them had spent six years and learned some English. They had come to start a laundry.

Second, Winnipeg had large Eastern European and Jewish populations that, unfortunately, were seen as a threat to the Anglo-British society. During World War I, Slavic immigrants lost their jobs, were disenfranchised, and landed in detention camps after being labelled enemy aliens. In 1919 violence erupted against German and Ukrainian immigrants as Winnipeg war veterans and hoodlums ransacked the North End. However, such harassment of Europeans did not mean the Chinese escaped unscathed.

It was jobs that drew the Chinese to Winnipeg, but they were in lowly service occupations. Eleven Chinese wash houses emerged during the 1890s.[2] Over the next two decades, newcomers surnamed Lee from Chen Shan village in Hoksan County arrived and dominated the laundry trade. They cut prices against competitors, and avoided working too close to one

*Pearl Wong Lee's mother travelling to Manitoba in 1915.*

another. They also blocked newcomers from entering the city: Chinese were stopped at the railway station, beaten and forced back onto the train. Eventually, representatives from the Lee family association came from the west coast to make peace.[3]

Clearly, the Lees of Hoksan County bonded with those of the same surname and home district rather than with every Chinese. In other Chinatowns, similar loyalties had prompted the rise of many organizations and helped in job searches, but without such violence as in Winnipeg.

Winnipeg's Chinese population grew slowly. In 1901 there were 100 men working in 29 laundries throughout the city. The first Chinese store, Quong Chong Tai, opened on King Street in 1905.

The city's population soared to 140,000 by 1911 amidst a burgeoning grain economy and rapid urban construction. The King and Alexander area thrived as a Chinatown. But health

*Chinese laundries in Winnipeg had red and white signs, 1995.*

officials frowned on crowded stores and bunkhouses, and took Chinese landlords to court on charges of overcrowding.[4]

By 1920 Winnipeg's 900 Chinese included eight families with 31 children. They ran 150 laundries along with three restaurants, eight Chinese grocery stores, and three coal-heated greenhouses.[5] Some Chinese sold fresh produce from door-to-door.

Laundries were the most visible aspect of the Chinese presence in the city, spread as they were throughout the city. A typical shop had a red and white sign in front, houseplants in the window, and bells over the door. Behind the counter stood shelves of clean laundry, folded and wrapped in paper. Further back were ironing tables and space for washing and drying. The kitchen, beds and toilet were at the very rear.

Most laundries had one to four workers. Laundry was brought from private homes in great bags by foot or wagon. These loads contained clothing, bed-sheets, tablecloths and napkins. Male customers dropped off shirts with detachable collars, which were starched before ironing.

Wood stoves boiled great vats of water, and then the laundry was soaked in the hot water. This heat offered one small consolation to the tough work: winter temperatures in Winnipeg could drop to forty below zero. All workers washed and ironed, but one person handled pick-up and delivery, another managed the kitchen, and the fellow who spoke the best English took care of the counter. Laundry was washed and dried three times a week, on Monday, Tuesday and Friday, and ironed twice a week, on Wednesday and Thursday. On Sundays, everyone went to Chinatown for a break.[6]

### Challenges to Self-Respect

Winnipeg's Chinese felt the sting of racism from the government and from fellow citizens. In line with views that Chinatown harboured "immoral" elements, law officers repeatedly cracked down on gambling and illegal liquor in Chinatown. For example, in May 1910 city police raided two gambling houses, arrested 28 men and marched them to the police station handcuffed in pairs. The men were quickly bailed out: the game-house keepers at $300 each, players at $100 each, and $50 for each onlooker. Prominent lawyers R.A. Bonnar, K.C. and A. Monkman defended the game-house keepers.

In such raids, Lee Hai, a Chinese "connected with the city detective force" assisted the police. Whether he was an interpreter, a police employee or an informer is unclear, but his fellow countrymen detested him. Once, when he entered a Chinatown store, the owner locked the door and reached for a large knife. But Lee Hai handily defended himself with a revolver. Of his enemies, the police said: "They have resorted to various devices, and have even gone so far as to have him put under bonds. They have attempted to bribe him and monies paid by Chinese in the spiriting away of witnesses have been turned into the court by Lee Hai, very much to the disappointment of his countrymen. ... Lee Hai's predecessor was intimidated to such a degree that the police had great difficulty in retaining his services until the conclusion of a number of cases then pending."[7]

In 1913 Manitoba banned Chinese from hiring white women. Whites who viewed Chinese café operators as "unfair competition" wanted them to hire white males and pay higher wages. Women's groups believed that Chinese employers might force female employees into sex or prostitution. This Manitoba law was never proclaimed by the Lieutenant-Governor-in-Council, however. In 1917 and 1919 Manitoba whites agitated for its enactment, but the Chinese Consul intervened successfully for the Chinese. In 1922 Winnipeg's Chinese Benevolent Association (CBA) called a meeting and decided to hire a lawyer and request consular help to proceed with protests. The CBA wanted every restaurant operator in Winnipeg to donate a tenth of their daily profits, and those elsewhere in the province to donate $5 each.[8]

Anti-Chinese racism occurred in many ways. Chinese were not allowed into theatres or dance halls. Individual laundrymen were bullied when they delivered or collected goods. White adults and children squeezed their noses closed while passing through Chinatown.[9] White Canadians derided Chinese fried noodles as "worms."[10] They often refused to pay for goods and services, shouting, "Fight you for the bill!" This meant the storekeeper would have to fight the customer and win in order to collect.[11] But as a minority lacking political clout, the Chinese could only maintain self-respect in silence.

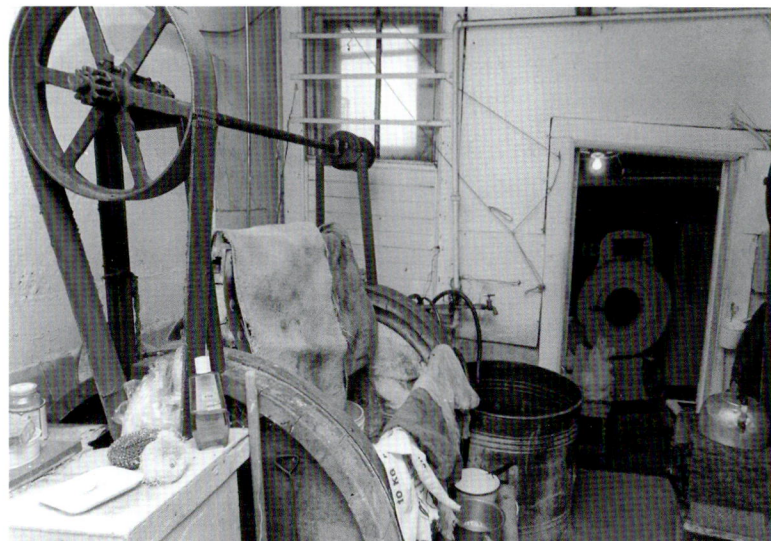

*A Winnipeg laundry in 1988 and a museum version of it in 2005.*

*Chinese Christian Association members at picnic, 1920.*

## Cease All Fighting

As elsewhere, Winnipeg's Chinese followed homeland politics, and their passions created conflicts. The Chinese Freemasons were formed in February 1911 to support revolutionary leader Dr. Sun Yat-sen, who visited in April. At the inauguration, a Chinese orchestra of 15 men played traditional instruments.

After the revolution, Fred Soo, Hoy Mon Ben, Joe Kimyou, Wong Toy and Wong Tu Wa created a branch of Dr. Sun's Kuomintang (KMT) in 1915. They represented Chinatown's merchant elite, because five associates from the firm McMeans and Wallar, which handled investments, real estate and legal advice for the Chinese, also attended the first meeting. Soon 150 Chinese had joined; four among them decided to publish the *People's Outlook* newspaper (*Min Shi Bao*).[12]

The KMT and Freemasons feuded bitterly. At the opening of the KMT branch, president Fred Soo called for local Chinese

"to work in co-operation, to cease all fighting among themselves, and to quit gambling."[13]

The plea for peace went unheeded. In 1915, when some men agitated for a third revolution in China and received a tepid response, they apparently made trouble everywhere.[14] They may or may not have been the same ones who, the following month, tried to extort funds from seven Chinatown merchants who were selling liquor without licences. When the merchants refused to pay, the extortionists informed the police, who confiscated the contraband and fined the merchants. As well, health inspectors checked Chinatown's stores when informants complained about sanitation there.[15]

In 1916 other Chinese formed a chapter of the Constitutionalist Party. With these three groups opposing one another, it proved difficult to set up a community-wide CBA. Failed attempts in 1917 were due to petty "financial problems." In 1918 CBA promoters had to counter rumours about their own trustworthiness, but a CBA emerged in 1919 and launched a Chinese language school.

China's northern government supported the Allies in World War I. But the local KMT supported Dr. Sun's southern government and sent a band to crash an outdoor display of Allied products. The band was chased away.[16] In 1923, as the Chinese exclusion law was being debated in Ottawa, a group tried to support national protest efforts. But local criticisms forced the group to shut down, but it still managed to raise $400 to send to Toronto.[17] In 1924, when 400 Chinese welcomed the Chinese consul general at a gathering, audience members denounced his northern origins.[18]

Two important community institutions were the church and a drama group. Christians had offered English lessons and religion since 1900 from St. Andrew's Presbyterian Church. Frank Fun and Wesley Lee formed a Chinese Young Men's

Christian Association (YMCA) in 1913. Two years later, English classes for the Chinese were underway at 12 different churches in the city. Class sizes ranged from 12 to 50.

In 1917 Reverend Mar Seung and Wong Soon Hong founded the Chinese Christian Association, supported by Presbyterians and Methodists. The latter purchased the Chinese Mission building on Logan Street with help from both Chinese and whites. The Mission hosted many activities, and the Chinese who used its address for mailing purposes dubbed it the Chinese Post Office. Although the Mission replaced the YMCA as the key beneficiary of Christian churches, the recreational facilities at the Y were used for reading and physical exercise until the 1930s.

During the 1920s the community continued to grow, even as Winnipeg's economy slowed down. Home district groups sprang up, as did clan associations for those surnamed Lee, Ma and Wong. In 1921 laundrymen Sun Wei and He Can formed the Jing Hun She (Vigilant Soul Society), a dramatic arts troupe. As many as thirty members gathered in evenings to practise singing and play musical instruments. The society staged Chinese operas and screened Chinese movies, often at the nearby Fox Theatre. One old-timer recalled:

> All those men dressed up as women. First they came from out of town. Late we had our own company. At first it was only twice a year, and we looked forward to it for months. Then it was once a week. Always a full house and sometimes the crowd would be out onto the street. We knew the stories by heart. They gave us some life, something to make us laugh and cry, to do something other than work. We were not allowed in the white man's cinema then you know, nor at social gatherings. Nothing for Chinese. We were totally separated from white people, except for doing business.[19]

In 2005, the Jing Hun She drama troupe was still active.

## Nothing Is More Dreadful

The Depression hit the prairies hard. As Winnipeg's Chinese went jobless, more turned to gambling. In September 1931, gunshots rang out one night in Chinatown, smashing windows, chipping walls, and piercing tin signs. The KMT president claimed that game-house operators were fighting KMT attempts to close the gambling houses. The KMT wanted to eliminate gambling for

*Jing Hun She (Chinese Dramatic Arts Society) musician, 1949.*

these reasons:

*The majority of the local Chinese work long hours in restaurants and laundries for small wages. They get paid on Saturday nights, go to the gambling houses, and usually lose all their money. Then they have nothing to send home to their families, nothing left with which to pay their dues to the societies they belong to, nothing for the organization which must some day ship their bodies back to China for burial in their native soil. Nothing is more dreadful for the Chinese than the thought of their graves being in a foreign land.[20]*

*Above: Jimmy Yee of Portage La Prairie training as a pilot in Winnipeg, 1933.*
*Below: $100 bond donation to China's Air Force, 1941.*

The KMT claimed its opponents had sent for "gunmen and hatchetmen" from Vancouver to help them. Fistfights followed, and combatants were arrested for assault and battery.[21] Despite more police patrols in the area, a tea merchant who belonged to the KMT was shot to death.[22]

During the 1930s the Chinese population shrank by a quarter. The number of Chinese grocery stores fell from 13 to 8 and, by 1939, only 19 laundries were still running, unlike the 150 of 20 years before.[23] As their shops closed, the Chinese moved so that by 1941, two-thirds of the city's Chinese lived in Chinatown.[24] The CBA distributed rice, helped restaurants get supplies from government-run kitchens, and helped others return to China.[25] The number of Chinese-run restaurants increased from 11 to 18 during this decade.[26]

When war between Japan and China started in 1937, feuding inside Winnipeg's Chinatown stopped. New groups such as the Chinese Patriotic League called for unity. Charlie Foo and W.J. Yuk of the Winnipeg KMT began raising funds for China's refugees and wounded soldiers. They offered to help pay the passage for any Chinese wanting to join China's armed forces. Local pilot Charles Wong, the "Oriental Wingbird," prepared to go to help fight Japan.

The war also united Chinese and some whites. In December 1937 the Chinese Patriotic League co-sponsored a forum at the Walker Theatre to denounce Japan. The Winnipeg Ministerial Association, the Trades and Labor Council, the Greater Winnipeg Young Liberals, the Winnipeg Youth Council and the Women's International League for Peace and Freedom all sent representatives, and noted Member of Parliament J.S. Woodsworth presided. At the meeting, the chair of the Chinese

Patriotic League pointed out that the Chinese were fighting not for themselves alone, but for the democracies of the entire world, where China's success or failure would greatly affect the West.[27] A collection that day took in $360 for the Chinese Red Cross.

Then fundraising intensified. Winnipeg's Chinese cancelled Chinese New Year celebrations. In 1939 they raised $2000 in one day for the Red Cross, enough to help 2000 refugees for an entire month.[28] Every Chinese in Winnipeg had to donate monthly or face public retribution. One reluctant donor was brought before a meeting of several hundred Chinese before he made good his donations the next day.[29] Funds went to airplanes for China, winter clothing for refugees, and relief for the home counties of Winnipeg's Chinese. They raised $130,000 during the war.[30]

**Can't Go Home**

Although Chinese immigration resumed after the war, Winnipeg's Chinatown stagnated. The residents were aging. "Within a few years, there won't be any Chinese in Winnipeg," said one person. "Myself, I am just about 50, and I am considered one of the younger Chinese in this city. Each year, many of them go back to China to spend their last days. Others, who cannot afford to go home, are gradually dying off."[31] Another factor was the small size of the original Chinese community, which led to slow growth in the 1950s.

But race relations improved in the press. In 1951 a reporter wrote sympathetically about the arrival of a son from China who had never met his father. That man approached 21-year-old Kay Wong at the train station and said, "You are my son."

"And you are my father," Kay replied.[32]

Another poignant news story told how 75-year-old Woo Wong, a partner in the Arlginton Laundry, had saved $1800 to return to China, only to lose the money during a visit to the Assiniboine Park zoo.[33]

The slow growth included foreign students and scholars. The Chinese Students Association began in 1953 with 100 members at the university, many of them students from Hong Kong. In 1959 teachers at the university formed the Manitoba Professional Club, which became the Manitoba Chinese Fellowship. It later helped with one early redevelopment plan for Chinatown.

In the meantime, Chinatown fell into the Cold War. In 1951 an Anti-Communist League was formed after reports surfaced of the Communists arresting people in south China and extorting money from their relatives in Canada. Winnipeg's old-timer merchants were allied with China's KMT government, based in Taiwan since 1949. During World War II, the KMT government had established a consulate in Winnipeg. In 1946 the KMT helped start a drum and bugle corps among the few Chinese families including Farns, Lees and Wongs.[34]

Of 15 Chinese families then in Winnipeg, five were of mixed race.[35] Not enough is known to say whether such marriages resulted from white women working for Chinese café owners, as was the case in Halifax.

Winnipeg's CBA had close ties with the KMT regime in Taiwan. In 1970 a CBA leader led delegates to Ottawa to oppose diplomatic recognition of China.

Five years later, the CBA arranged for Winnipeg politicians to visit Taichung, a Taiwanese city twinned to Winnipeg in 1971. The twinning occurred after Canada's diplomatic recognition of China, so Ottawa barred the delegation and refused to recognize the tie.

**You Work and Work**

In the 1960s Chinatown's situation was discouraging. The CBA fought off an attempt to put an extension of the nearby Disraeli

*During a 1939 Royal Visit, Winnipeg's Chinese joined city-wide celebrations.*

Freeway through Chinatown. Still, only 200 seniors among Winnipeg's 3000 Chinese lived there. The KMT's membership fell from 300 to 100, and young Chinese left in search of better wages. Rundown buildings lost fire insurance coverage and were torn down. Hong Kong investors travelled through in 1968, but locals doubted they would invest here.[36]

The following year, Chinatown was designated an urban renewal area, and qualified for government assistance. A Chinatown Development Corporation drew up plans for a closed mall with shopping, living, entertainment and recreational areas. The five-stage project would eventually cover all Chinatown. But plans stalled when area merchants—owners of restaurants, grocery stores and small import companies—couldn't raise $2 million, their share of the $10 million project.

The old establishment members were resistant. They scorned the educated newcomers[37] who arrived in such high numbers as immigration from Hong Kong rose through the 1970s. When the Manitoba Chinese Fellowship published a directory of Chinese residents in 1977, 10,000 Chinese were listed as living in 38 Manitoba communities. [38] A new middle class organized in Winnipeg around culture and education,

and it challenged the CBA, complaining that the organization was undemocratic and slow to change.[39] In 1976 three new groups demanded that the CBA change the way it ran the Chinese pavilion during Folklorama, the annual multicultural festival. The CBA refused, so the groups withdrew their support. Three years later, they mounted an alternate pavilion.

By the late 1970s Chinese lived throughout Winnipeg, almost half of them in four areas. Chinatown housed seniors with low incomes, both newcomers and pre-1923 old-timers. High-income families, headed by managers or professionals, lived in Fort Richmond. The downtown periphery contained Chinese of mixed age groups, many homeowners, and middle-income earners. Finally, many foreign students lived in the River-Osborne and Pembina Highway areas, near the universities.[40] This population could see Chinese movies at a theatre, listen to a Chinese radio program each week, or read a local newspaper, the *Manitoba Chinese Post*.

Newcomers to Winnipeg sought to fill the niche of serving Chinese food to non-Chinese. The number of restaurants grew during the 1970s, multiplying from 15 in 1968 to 70 in 1979. Restaurant ownership changed frequently. One operator explained why:

*"To open a restaurant?" It is not worthwhile. There are a thousand things that you have to watch out [for] as if they were your last chance. You think of the food, fuel, customers, waiters, health inspectors and grocery dealers. … You do the waiter's work when he is not around. You do dishwashing when no one else will. You work and work just to make ends meet. Then there are those students. They don't turn up if they have exams, and they don't turn up if they have dates. I would much rather work for someone else. If I am sick of working for one boss, I can simply pack up and go to another. Never again.[41]*

## For Future Local People

In 1979–80 Manitoba received 4000 Southeast Asian refugees, including many ethnic Chinese. With 2600 refugees coming to Winnipeg, the Chinese population was boosted to over 6000 and invigorated Chinatown. This coincided with the Core Area Initiatives, funded by the three levels of government to fix up Winnipeg's inner city.

By then, Chinatown had two new projects. In 1978 the Chinese United Church had erected the $2.5 million Sek On Toi, 88-units of senior citizens housing, largely to replace two buildings of seniors' housing destroyed by fires in 1969 and 1972. And private developers built a shopping plaza at King and Alexander Streets.

A new Chinatown Development (1981) Corporation was formed. Subsequent plans for Chinatown included a public garden, street landscaping of King Street, an underground parking lot, a cultural centre, low-cost family housing and a gate.

Internal dissent arose again. Some Chinese considered the old Chinatown site inappropriate, given nearby Main Street's crime and alcoholism. They preferred a centre in suburban Fort Garry or Tuxedo or River Heights. Others doubted the government funds would arrive. Insiders suggested that the community had two separate components that occupied separate worlds: immigrants who lived around Chinatown, and professionals who didn't.[42]

As well, the proposed Chinese Cultural and Community Services Centre (CCCSC) needed funds from either fundraising or private developers. When the latter was chosen, the corporation was criticized as providing unfair advantage to one group.[43] The Chinese garden, gate, street landscaping, and low-cost housing were completed in 1986. The following year, the CCCSC opened in the Dynasty Building.

A driving force at the CCCSC was Dr. Joseph Du, an ethnic Chinese who had grown up in Vietnam, studied in Taiwan and married a French-Canadian nurse. In his job, he frequently flew out to remote First Nations reserves in northern Manitoba to provide medical services. He organized help for Vietnamese refugees in 1979, and received the Order of Canada in 1985. Dr. Du also ran as a candidate in the 1984 federal election, hoping to spark more political involvement from ethnic groups.

Also key to Chinatown's revival was businessman Ken Wong. He had been elected to Winnipeg City Council in 1974, and later headed the Chinatown Non-Profit Hous-ing Corporation. He had a strong vision for Chinatown:

> The basis for the area's economy must be refugees and the new immigrants. Right now there's nothing to keep them here. We want a solid basis for those people to stay. What I don't want to see is building a community centre for us groups in Tuxedo, Fort Garry and River Heights. We've got to build for local people and future local people as well as for us.[44]

In the mid-1980s, Chinese immigrants and off-shore money were viewed as important stimulants to sluggish Manitoba. In 1985 the province opened an office in Hong Kong to attract capital investment. A year later, 25 Hong Kong immigrants in the Entrepreneur category came to Manitoba to invest

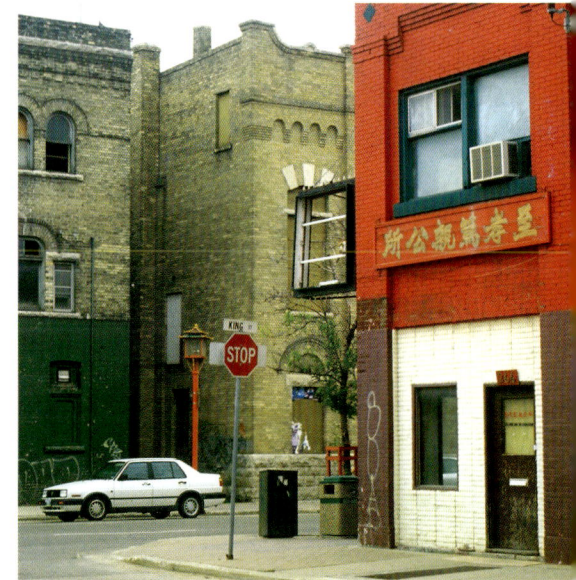

*Chinatown is in the old part of Winnipeg, 2004.*

over $12 million, creating 136 new jobs.

There were other success stories. Mack Chang, a Chinese refugee from Laos, opened his second hardware, lumber and building materials store on Logan Avenue in 1985. The following year, Wah Loong (Winnipeg) Limited, a joint venture with Hong Kong's Sun Wah Group, invested $1 million in wholesale seafood distribution. Other immigrants set up supermarkets, beauty shops, even a Chinese and Kosher restaurant (at the Viscount Gort Flag Inn). Prosperity Knitwear of Winnipeg had 40 employees, and Dynabright Canada launched the first dye house in western Canada for Winnipeg's garment industry.[45]

By 1988 the difficulties of doing business in Winnipeg had become apparent. Many Entrepreneur immigrants had entered the restaurant and retail sectors, which involved less capital and fewer new jobs. One Hong Kong immigrant who had started an import/export business in agricultural products found the Canadian market smaller than expected. Transportation costs were higher for businesses involved with the Pacific Rim market, while Winnipeg's smaller population tested the abilities of business owners. When a number of Entrepreneur immigrants left for Vancouver and Toronto, the Business immigration co-ordinator for Manitoba put part of the blame on the harsh climate: "The reality of life here is that it's cold here in the winter."[46]

### The "Winnipeg Connection"

In 2001 Winnipeg's Chinese population of 11,000 was outnumbered by South Asians (15% of visible minorities), African Canadians (14%) and Filipinos (36%). The Chinese were only 13% of the city's visible minorities (which in turn formed 12% of the citizenry). Still, they boasted a number of organizations including the Manitoba Academy of Chinese Studies (which ran language classes and a choir), several Chinese-language churches, and several martial arts schools. The local dragon-boat races, however, were organized by the Canadian Cancer Society as a fundraising event.

In 2001 four groups—the Jewish Heritage Centre of Western Canada, Jewish Federation of Winnipeg, Manitoba Japanese Canadian Citizens Association and Winnipeg Chinese Cultural and Community Centre—co-sponsored "Shanghai Connection." This exhibit described how 18,000 Jews reached safety in Shanghai after Chinese and Japanese diplomats in Nazi-occupied Europe issued them travel documents. The show also profiled three Winnipeg families descended from the Shanghai refugees. The "Winnipeg connection" was key to this project, given the city's large Jewish community.

*Winnipeg Chinese Cultural and Community Centre, 2004.*

# 5

# TORONTO: BUSY, BUSY, BUSY

*Busy Chinatown market, 1980.*

The intersection of Spadina Avenue and Dundas Street marks the heart of Toronto's largest Chinatown. Three of the corners hold branches of the Big Five banks, while Asian banks are also nearby. At each change of the traffic signals, a crowd of residents, tourists, shoppers and children surges onto the road. Businesses stretch for several blocks, displaying bright signage in Chinese, Vietnamese and English.

This face is Chinatown's most visible. Stores sell live crabs on sidewalks packed with bins of fruits and greens, racks of colourful T-shirts, and displays of trinkets. Loudspeakers play Chinese opera and Asian pop while the sharp smells of natural medicines drift from herb stores. You could be strolling in Asia, where merchandise spills onto the streets of shopping areas.

Post-1967 immigrants created this centre of Canada's largest Chinese community. Glance at the buildings' second and third storeys, and you'll

*Toronto-bound Chinese coming from the United States and passing through Sarnia, 1897.*

find the red brick, arched windows and pilasters of Victorian architecture. The newcomers are recycling buildings left by the Jews when their community moved north. At the same time, immigrant Chinese investment spurred the construction of new shopping malls, condominium high-rises and storefronts.

This district is in Toronto's busy urban core. Located close to universities, the Art Gallery of Ontario, the Eaton Centre, the financial district and the Skydome, Chinatown also has a local residential base. Its side streets are lined with restored Victorian houses, schools, mature trees and neat gardens along with traditional Chinese organizations.

Toronto's Chinatown stayed small for many years. At first, this reflected the small number of jobs open to Chinese people. When the federal government halted Chinese immigration in 1923, Toronto was home to 2100 Chinese. With postwar immigration changes, this number gradually rose to 6700 by the early 1960s. From then on, Toronto's triumph as Canada's business engine and lead metropolis attracted a steady flow of Chinese immigrants from around the world. They outnumbered those landing in Vancouver, and created several Chinatowns in the Greater Toronto Area (GTA).

## Laundries Again

It is surmised that the earliest Chinese came to Toronto from the south because the city's first Chinese laundries emerged in 1877, the same year that American Chinese reached Montreal and Winnipeg. They may have migrated because of the depression of the mid-1870s, when a million people abandoned the eastern United States to head for California.[1] Some American Chinese may have preferred to go north, given California's anti-Chinese fervour.

Toronto's Chinese were few in number but industrious. By 1881 there were 10 Chinese-run laundries downtown.[2] The tally stayed low: a decade later saw only 24 Chinese washhouses, but they were 43 percent of all laundries.[3] By 1900 the number of Chinese laundries had quadrupled, and 150–200 Chinese lived in Toronto. They also ran a restaurant, two dry goods and vegetable stores, and several tea stores downtown.[4]

## The "Yellow Peril"

Even as a sliver of the city's population, the Chinese faced racial hostility that targeted their work. In 1902 Toronto passed a bylaw to regulate and inspect laundries, similar to laws in Vancouver and Calgary. At the same time, the Toronto Trades and Labour Council wanted Asians excluded from Canada or a $1000 head tax.[5] In 1915, white laundrymen urged the public to boycott Chinese laundries and pressed city hall to cancel those licences. In response, the Chinese pooled funds to protect their interests.[6]

Ontario legislated against Chinese employers in 1914, forbidding them to hire white women. The Chinese in Toronto raised funds for a legal battle, but the government's ban was delayed when a Chinese café owner in Moose Jaw challenged a similar Saskatchewan law. His case reached the Supreme Court of Canada but was defeated, whereupon the Ontario law came into effect in 1920.

In 1918 Torontonian whites demanded that city hall withhold business licences from laundrymen and restaurant operators lacking Canadian citizenship, another move to reduce Chinese competition. The Chinese consul went to city hall to defend his countrymen, and repeated the trip when the same proposal arose again in later years.[7]

Local magazines, some respectable and others less so, portrayed the Chinese in a stereotypical and negative light. Sometimes writers singled out specific "evils":

> The Chinaman will always adhere to his own customs … already they are grouping themselves together and congregating into a district that will soon be entirely their own where gambling (a weakness natural to all Chinamen), opium smoking and other vices may be carried on with small fear of interruption.[8]

Other articles alluded to a vague threat:

> One need only stroll through the above mentioned block [King, Queen, Yonge and York Streets] and notice the throngs of Chinamen lounging in the streets and doorways to realize the 'Yellow Peril' is more than a mere word in this city. The average citizen would stand aghast did he but realize the awful menace lurking behind the partitions or screens of some of these innocent appearing laundries and restaurants.[9]

This blatant hostility formed the background to Chinese life in Toronto.

## Oriented Towards China

Early on, Christian influences were evident. Men from the YMCA classes of the 1880s started the Chinese Christian Endeavour Society, which promoted contacts with China through famine relief and missionary support.[10] By 1910 almost half of Toronto's 1000 Chinese attended classes at Christian churches. That year, the Chinese Christian Association was founded by Presbyterians. Not only did this mission provide language classes, a reading room, lodging to students from China and a kindergarten for local families[11] but it also acted as a leader in the absence of a formal Chinese benevolent association. The mission's members attended conferences of Chinese in eastern Canada and the American northeast.[12]

In 1923 the mission's successor, the Young Men's Christian Institute (YMCI) rallied against the bill before Parliament to end Chinese immigration. A group with cross-country reach operated from the YMCI and held a conference at Victoria Hall. A thousand people came from Chinese communities across Ontario and Canada. In the

Quong Lock ran a grocery story and a laundry in Toronto, 1921.

DOMINION OF CANADA
**DEPARTMENT OF IMMIGRATION AND COLONIZATION**
CHINESE IMMIGRATION SERVICE

C. I.
45

George Thomas Sing Wah Lock
NO. 45426

This is to certify that 278 Spadina Ave., Toronto, Ontario.

whose photograph is attached hereto, has

registered as required by Section 18 of the

Chinese Immigration Act, Chapter 38,

13-14 George V.

Dated at Ottawa, Ontario.

this 20th day of June 1924

Controller of Chinese Immigration.
This certificate does not establish legal status in Canada.

*All Chinese Canadians, even eight-year-old Tom Lock, had to register with the government in 1923.*

committee of eight that went to lobby Ottawa, three members were from Toronto.[13]

China's politics also surfaced. In 1903 the Chinese Empire Reform Association emerged in Toronto, to be followed by the Chinese Freemasons. When Dr. Sun was in Toronto in 1911 to speak, he received painful news about the failed Yellow Flower Hill uprising in Guangzhou, where 72 of his followers died. After Dr. Sun's revolution succeeded, his KMT also emerged in Toronto.

The KMT and the Freemasons were fierce opponents in Toronto as elsewhere. They squabbled over aid funds: should the money go to the Northern regime or to Dr. Sun?[14] The

Freemasons probably cheered when Canada shut down the KMT newspaper *Shing Wah* and arrested ten KMT members in 1918. After *Shing Wah* resumed publishing in 1922, the Freemasons launched their own newspaper, the *Hung Zhong Bao*. A few years later, the editor at one newspaper sued his counterpart for slandering his wife.[15]

By 1923, when Chinese immigration was banned, Toronto's Chinese had formed organizations — two based on home districts and ten based on clans. The Lees, Maks, Lams, Wongs and Chans were most numerous.

The strongest passions were aroused by China's crises. In response to the 1925 "Shanghai Incident," a thousand angry Chinese rallied in Toronto and raised funds for the victims. The Freemasons formed the Resist Japan Association in 1928, after Japan stepped up its bullying of China. The Ontario Patriotic Association raised money to buy six airplanes, which were crated and shipped to China. When war broke out between China and Japan in 1937, China dispatched an agent to Toronto, the headquarters for fundraising in Ontario. The first meeting of the Chinese Patriotic Federation's at the Carr Cinema on Queen Street lasted two days.[16]

A flurry of activities followed, including a flying school for Chinese youth and tag days on city streets. China opened an embassy in Toronto. Local Chinese worked alongside non-Chinese groups such as the Red Cross and the Chinese War Relief Fund, an organization that raised over $4 million, mostly from white Canadians.[17] After the war, the Chinese Patriotic Federation became the Chinese Community Centre of Ontario, a Chinese benevolent association (CBA). Its KMT roots led to its support for Taiwan and opposition to Communist China.

**One Day Off**

In the 1910s Chinatown gradually claimed Queen Street's

south side, between York and Elizabeth.[18] Earlier police harassment had kept the Chinese "on the move" and delayed Chinatown's start.[19] In the following decade, Chinatown expanded to Queen Street's north side and then north along Elizabeth Street to Dundas and into the former Jewish area.[20] This was "Old Chinatown," and its businesses struggled to survive:

> My dad sold everything. He was a full-fledged herbalist and he had a cabinet of herbs at the back of the store. He had an ice-box and he sold meat. He sold all the Chinese groceries which he imported. He had a stove in the centre towards the back, and he used to make his own Chinese sausage on a sausage-making machine.
>
> He sold to laundries and restaurants from the truck. Everybody did. You had store business and truck business. The only time you went to Chinatown was on Sunday because they had the one day off. If they ran out of groceries in the middle of the week, they couldn't afford to go to Chinatown because they had to work from 6–7 a.m. to midnight. My dad would go out two or three times a week on a circuit. He had to deliver because a bag of rice was 45 pounds, a barrel of soap was 120 pounds, a barrel of starch was 120 pounds, and a bag of soda, 100 pounds. You couldn't take that on the streetcar very well.[21]

Thirteen Chinese families lived in Chinatown in the 1930s, while others resided in other neighbourhoods, usually behind or above the restaurants or laundries run by the household. Chinatown was the focal point of the community, where opera groups practised, churches provided services and the Canadian-born gathered. The gambling houses not only offered distractions to its customers but also provided jobs and shelter to the unemployed. One man commented, "They served the same purposes as the churches, Salvation Army and employment agencies."

The lack of families was apparent to all, as one man who had been in Canada for 62 years recalled:

> I remember looking out over the big dining room of our restaurant on a busy day in 1946. I counted one hundred old Chinese men sitting out there and just six women, four Chinese and two Canadian. And I thought to myself, if Canadian culture has a Christian spirit, how could they deny Chinese their families? The whole city of Toronto didn't have a dozen Chinese women in 1946. You know, they talk a lot about the Chinese gambling and all those things, but don't forget, this was all there was to do.[22]

In the mid-1950s, city officials destroyed Old Chinatown, taking most of it for a new city hall and civic square.

*Peddler selling live chickens in Chinatown, 1926.*

*Immigrant women taking English lessons, 1959.*

Considered an ugly blight on the urban landscape, Chinatown's rooming houses and apartments were bulldozed. But while housing was reduced, the Chinese population climbed (to 6700 by 1961) as the wives and descendants of the old-timer Chinese arrived with the repeal of the exclusion legislation. With intimate ties to Old Chinatown, the old-timer Chinese and their families moved into the adjacent area bounded by Dundas, Spadina, College and University Avenues. Newcomers who didn't speak English liked Chinatown, and jobs were available in nearby garment factories.

"New Chinatown" was formerly a Jewish district of shops, businesses and two- and three-storey houses dating from the mid- and late nineteenth century. Many of its stately homes had belonged to the city's ruling elite. Immigration to Toronto skyrocketed after 1967 as newcomers chose Ontario over British Columbia. Businesses expanded along the streets of New Chinatown, while a few stores and restaurants stayed in Old Chinatown. Both districts struggled to survive.

## Saving Old Chinatown

Old Chinatown had suffered from long years of physical neglect. After the new City Hall opened in 1965, Toronto's development commissioner wanted to demolish the remainder of Old Chinatown for another civic square. However, Torontonians proved fond of Old Chinatown, and called for it to be saved. This downtown land was valuable: speculators had driven prices from $12 a square foot to over $30 within a year. But city hall was indifferent or hostile: one committee chair said preserving Chinatown would only turn it into a ghetto.

Mrs. Jean Lumb, restaurant owner and activist, argued Old Chinatown's case:

> One reason why we feel there should always be a China-town in a city the size of Toronto is simply that there has been one, and to have it lost would be strongly felt. Its existence has its effects on people, especially as long as there are new Chinese immigrants coming every year.
>
> We should have a spot for them to start from, a place where they can be among their own people, hear their own language spoken. The Chinese people are quiet and reserved; it takes them longer than many other immigrants to make friends, to get used to new ways.
>
> Some people say a Chinatown encourages ghettos and this is a reason why it shouldn't be, but that's not so. It just gives the people a sense of belonging. It's a nice environment for them until they're ready to go on their way more and fit into the Canadian community.[23]

A Save Chinatown Committee emerged and in 1969 the city endorsed keeping Old Chinatown. Help came from United Action of Chinese Canadians (UACC), formed two years earlier by students and young professionals from Hong Kong, and from the Chinese Canadian Association, a group of Canadian-born Chinese. But Chinatown wasn't safe yet. In 1970, the city proposed widening Dundas Street to six lanes, which would have sliced into the shops of Old Chinatown. UACC protests helped quash the proposal. But when metropolitan Toronto officials revived it in 1975, Toronto City Council itself rejected it.

**How Many Chinatowns?**

Meanwhile, neighbouring New Chinatown also fought to retain its residential nature. The Toronto Planning Board wanted to let the University of Toronto expand into it in 1969. But the plan died when student enrolment fell. Then the board wanted to zone the area for high-density residential, commercial and institutional use. When the Chinese Canadian Association and UACC protested, the city set up the 'South East Spadina Ad Hoc Steering Committee' to help create zoning plans.

While the committee did its work, other issues arose. The Spadina Expressway threatened to run through Toronto's older neighbourhoods, including New Chinatown. Only a determined fight by community groups stopped it. As well, Ontario Hydro demolished an entire block of houses for a 12-storey transformer station. Residents complained to the city, which supported their bid for low-income housing. In 1973 city council approved the low-density zoning proposed by the steering committee, which helped stabilize the area.

But when this zoning blocked plans for a Dundas and Spadina site, its developers challenged the ad-hoc committee. The developers rallied merchants, and Chinese groups formed a rival Planning Association and declared the ad-hoc committee unrepresentative. When the city ordered changes to the committee's membership, local residents and tenants (both Chinese and non-Chinese) formed the Grange Community Coalition. It was led by a group called Chinese Canadians for Mutual Advancement, containing Hong Kong students and social workers who helped working class immigrants.

The stakes were high. At a crucial election, a coalition member reported:

> We were disrupted by boos, jeers, shouts, screams, obscene and sexist remarks and generally extremely crude and vulgar behavior from the cheering mob brought in by the Chinatown Planning Association. … When votes for Mrs. Chow were called for, threats were heard like 'Those who don't raise their hands are traitors to the Han race!'[24]

Hong Kong immigrants—businesspeople and social workers, workers in Chinatown and residents of Chinatown West—were on both sides of this pitched battle. When neither side would budge, the city imposed a compromise solution in 1978. High-density commercial and housing development (which the developers sought) would be allowed along parts of Spadina Avenue, subject to review by city planners. The plan also kept overall residential aspects as well as the low-density

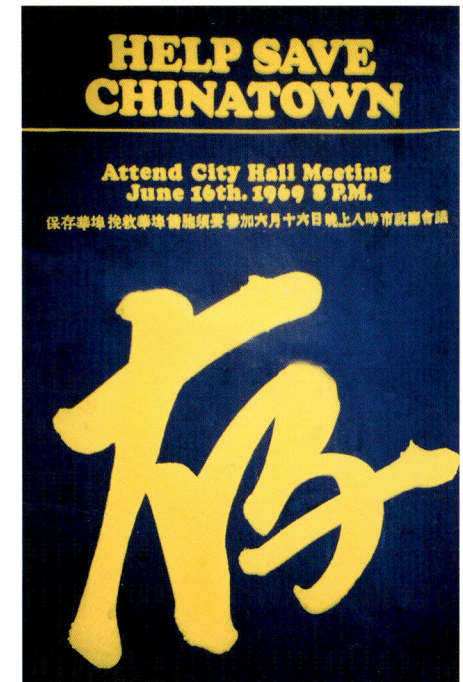

*Rallying the community, 1969.*

commercial areas on Dundas Avenue. Neither side in the battle, however, was happy with this outcome.[25]

When immigrants moved beyond Old and New Chinatown, the tension between developers and residents resurfaced as entrepreneurs set up shops and restaurants in East Chinatown, Scarborough, Markham and Richmond Hill over the next thirty years.

Around 1972 a third Chinatown emerged in the Broadview-Gerrard area, an old working-class district east of downtown. Its house prices and rents were low, and the area had large parks, schools, a public library and good public transit. As this Chinatown prospered, nearby residents complained about sanitation and parking. They wanted residential zoning, but merchants won low-density commercial zoning. By the mid-1980s "Chinatown East" was bigger than Old Chinatown, but still smaller than New Chinatown.[26]

In 1994 local residents around Chinatown East petitioned for a development freeze. A third of the 500 signatures were Chinese. Merchants issued a counter-petition that garnered 1100 supporters, insisting that Chinatown benefited the overall economy. Others felt the Chinese were scapegoats for the overall lack of parking. Some people thought complaints about Chinatown were racist; others viewed the clash as between commercial and residential interests and not about Chinese versus non-Chinese.[27]

Settlement had pushed out to the suburbs when well-to-do newcomers arrived, and earlier immigrants wanted larger homes. In Scarborough, then a city east of Toronto, Chinese shops opened in Torchin Plaza, across from two existing plazas. By 1984 Chinese firms dominated all three plazas, which became known as Agincourt Chinatown and flourished due to lower rents and the local Chinese residents.

*Toronto's Chinese Cultural Centre is in Scarborough (top), as is the Dragon Centre, one of many Asian malls in the region, 2004.*

When the roller-skating rink at one of the plazas was rebuilt as Dragon Centre with a 350-seat restaurant and 20 stores, Agincourt Chinatown attracted customers from across Toronto. In May 1984, 500 residents attended a meeting where complaints about traffic problems escalated into an anti-Chinese, anti-immigration frenzy. Later that year, a pamphlet arrived at 400 homes, alleging that Hong Kong immigrants were linked to criminal activities in their homeland and asking residents to demand that the government change its "open" immigration policy. In response, the Chinese in Scarborough formed the Federation of Chinese Canadians in Scarborough (FCCS) to counter the charges, and Scarborough city council passed a motion that condemned the pamphlet. The city had already set up a Task Force on Multiculturalism and Race Relations in 1983.

Two years later, when another Chinese mall containing a 440-seat theatre and a 130-seat restaurant was proposed, local residents again anticipated traffic congestion, parking problems and the loss of non-Chinese stores. But this time, protesters deliberately distanced themselves from racists. The local community association president indicated that any movie theatre would attract cars, no matter whether it was either of the big chain cinemas, Odeon or Famous Players.

Even Chinese residents opposed the proposal. The FCCS president told city council: "We are getting fed up with being caught in the crossfire between the developers and ratepayers time and again." Chinese businesspeople were told to act responsibly instead of causing problems for the entire community.[28] The FCCS president also pointed to a double standard: "They say Chinese should not cling together, but what about white enclaves like Forest Hill and Leaside?"[29]

When another incident of anti-Chinese hate literature occurred in Scarborough in 1991, the community blamed the local government for its lack of action.[30]

*Chinese restaurant/shop displaying roast meats, 2001*

Chinese settlement spread further north into towns such as Markham and Richmond Hill. In March 1994, a 137-unit Asian shopping mall proposed for south Richmond Hill drew local opposition, even from Chinese residents. When Richmond Hill altered its Official Plan and passed an interim bylaw reducing the number of units allowed in such projects, the developer appealed to the Ontario Municipal Board (OMB), a quasi-judicial body that settles land-use disputes. Then concerns around Chinese immigration exploded.

In June 1995 Markham town councillor Carol Bell said that new housing was being marketed solely to the Chinese, their malls lacked English-language signs, and there was too much retail space. She claimed these problems had caused longtime residents, the backbone of the community, to leave. When outraged Chinese residents demanded an apology, Bell refused.

*Chinatown, late 1990s*

A Chinese spokesperson pointed out: "If development is happening too fast, then council can deal with that issue. But to point a finger at one ethnic group is unfair."[31]

As the story heated up, it made news headlines across Canada and in Hong Kong.

A Chinese newspaper poll in Toronto found that 60 percent of 700 respondents agreed with Bell that development was too rapid. But 70 percent also felt she had raised the issue in a racist way. "It's not what she said about development, it's how she linked it with the backbone of the community leaving," said one observer. "We pay taxes. We help support this community."[32]

When Richmond Hill's Official Plan became permanent in September, the developer alleged his project had suffered from the racism of town officials. A former leader of the CCNC argued that smaller retail units were vital to immigrants who had little capital or luck in finding work.[33] The current CCNC president labelled Richmond Hill's actions as racist because they disproportionately affected Chinese businesses.[34] In the end, the OMB struck down Richmond Hill's actions, but aligned itself with residents by imposing fewer units, less restaurant space and more parking on the development. This halted the project.[35] Again, these tensions did not expressly represent white versus Chinese interests specifically, but arose from residential versus commercial interests.

These events reflected the rapid spread of Chinese Canadians through the GTA, with concentrations in Scarborough, Markham and Richmond Hill. And while many Chinese lived in the suburbs, the downtown Chinatowns still thrived.

**Toronto the Good**

By 1991 the Chinese immigrants in Greater Toronto Area (GTA) were of widely diverse origins: Hong Kong (40%), China

(30%), Vietnam (10%), other Asian countries (9%), Taiwan (4%), and the West Indies (3%). Names in the news represented all these home countries. For example, Dr. Joseph Wong of Hong Kong was named Man of the Year for his volunteer work with seniors' health care and the United Way. Developer Domingo Penaloza was one of 10,000 Filipino Chinese living in the Toronto area.[36] Tony Wong, born in Jamaica, reported for the *Toronto Star* newspaper. Literary critic Lien Chao is from China.

Among the post-1967 immigrants, many spoke English, were educated and highly qualified for professional jobs. Others were not, and worked in Chinatown where an abundant labour supply let employers pay low wages and hire and fire at will. At one such establishment, a restaurant with Hong Kong owners, the workers opted for unionization. When the owners demanded a share of the tips, previously pooled and divided among the staff, three Hong Kong immigrants approached the United Food and Commercial Workers Union (UFCWU), and signed up 70 percent of the restaurant staff.

The owners claimed workers had been coerced and didn't know what they had signed. Following hearings at the Labour Board, a union was certified, but it faded away when management backed off from the tips and stalled contract talks. Two of the three organizers quit because of harassment, and other workers lost hope.[37]

The garment industry saw job losses and oppressive work conditions in the late 1990s. Manufacturers competing against cheaper Free Trade products had to close their factories. Between 1988 and 1995, Toronto lost half of all its garment jobs.[38] Companies then subcontracted work to home seamstresses and to small shops where low wages and sweatshop work conditions were common.

In 1999 home-sewing in Toronto involved 8000 people, of which 60 percent were Chinese or Vietnamese. Paid by the piece, these women were supposed to get $7.54 an hour (10 percent over minimum wage for supplying machines and electricity), but they actually received $5 or $6 an hour. Some earned as little as $2 an hour. "I know I'm being underpaid, but there is nothing I can do," said Ching (a pseudonym). "If I don't do it someone else will. The boss knows where to get cheap labour."[39]

Many of these piece workers were refugees with no status. New groups arose to support them. For example, the Mainland Chinese Refugee Organization (MCRO) was started in 1991 for those who had failed to gain refugee status to stay in Canada. In 1993 the MCRO tried to win support from existing Chinese organizations. Its first issue was strategic: should the MCRO highlight China's bleak human rights or should it focus on its members' contributions to Canada?

The MCRO realized the first option risked alienating pro-China interests within the Chinese communities, as well as the Canadian government (which also valued business ties with China). The MCRO surveyed its members and found that 80 percent had at least high school education, 62 percent did not rely on welfare, and none had criminal records. When this information was released, the Chinese mass media finally portrayed the refugee claimants in a positive light.[40]

Diversity was also seen in political allegiances. Gordon Chong, elected to Toronto City Council in 1982, presided over the Chinese Canadian Progressive Conservative Association. Olivia Chow, school board trustee and Metro Toronto councillor, had strong ties to the New Democratic Party. And Robert Wong, Ontario's first Chinese-Canadian cabinet minister, was a Liberal.

Toronto shared two trends with Vancouver that set the larger urban centres apart: trends in the arts and political activism.

Toronto Chinese Chamber Orchestra Presents

# FOU TS'ONG

Piano Recital All-Chopin Programme

博聰

蕭邦作品演奏會

*Pianist Fou Ts'ong was internationally renowned for performing western classics.*

In Toronto, the development of the arts reflected the great diversity of media and arts institutions in the city as well as the critical mass of population. Some artistic practices focused on preserving and sharing traditional expressions such as Chinese music, opera or calligraphy. These were supported by many groups such as the Chinese Cultural Centre of Greater Toronto.

At the same time, new talent emerged. Author Judy Fong Bates (*Midnight at the Dragon Café*) wrote about immigrant life in small town Ontario while Terry Woo (*banana boys*) portrayed the lives of Toronto yuppies in the late 1990s. Filmmakers Keith Lock and Richard Fung respectively explored the lives of foreign Chinese students and gay Asians. Toronto's theatre scene witnessed plays such as *Bachelor Man* (by Winston Kam), which examined reaction to the 1923 exclusion law and *Mother Tongue* (by Betty Quan), which probed family issues. Composer Chan Ka Nin's opera *Iron Road* and Young People's Theatre's *Ghost Train* premiered in Toronto in 2001; both used Chinese-Canadian actors, singers and musicians. The arts let ethnic communities challenge stereotypes of themselves, criticize the mainstream, and continue to define an ethnic identity.

While Toronto became the most multicultural city in the world, it also witnessed intense ethnic unrest. It experienced subway violence directed at South Asians, right-wing extremists, and defacing of Jewish synagogues. African-Canadians protested a Royal Ontario Museum exhibit and the 1993 revival of the musical *Showboat* as being insulting and racist. Between 1988 and 1992, eight young people of Caribbean origin were killed by the police, seemingly without just cause. These grievances erupted in the Yonge Street riot that followed the Rodney King verdict (police were acquitted of beating him) in California in 1992.

Issues around racism, equality and equity also arose. Dora Nipp and the Toronto Association for Democracy in China called for support for human rights in China. Lawyer Susan Eng challenged the police establishment by pressing for public accountability during her term on the Police Services Board. Avvy Go of the Southeast Asian Legal Clinic spoke out on many immigrant issues. Winnie Ng denounced abuses of immigrant workers and worked for the International Ladies' Garment Workers Association. Physician Alan Li led advocacy groups such as the Chinese Canadian National Council and Gay Asians of Toronto. Concerns focused on the most vulnerable and most marginalized: refugee claimants, undocumented immigrants, gays and lesbians.

The Chinese communities were part of the great change that dramatically transformed Toronto in the last half century. Up until the 1960s, it had been Toronto the Good. Its people had been British, Protestant and supporters of the Crown. God-fearing and church-going, they had disdained pleasure-seeking and made it illegal to gamble and difficult to buy liquor. Toronto was a clean and orderly city where modesty and respectability were important values.

After World War II, the transformation was driven by immigration: from Italy, then Greece, Hungary, Uganda (South Asians), the Caribbean, and Asia. By 2001, the percentage of recent immigrants (44%) was among the highest in the world's large cities. These people gave Toronto vibrant neighbourhoods such as Greektown, Little Italy, India Bazaar, and several Chinatowns. The urban landscape showed signage in many languages, new consumer services such as wine bars, Chinese malls and sidewalk cafés, and architecturally distinct places of worship. Fine dining and nightlife opportunities increased, and residents grew confident as they embraced a cosmopolitan sensibility.

*Chinatown signs, late 1990s.*

# 6

# OTTAWA: LATE BLOOMER

*Somerset Street, 2004.*

Ottawa's Chinatown is in a district officially known as Somerset Heights. It is not exclusively Chinese, but is shared with firms run by Canadians from the Middle East, Korea, Japan, India and Vietnam. In the past, the neighbourhood around Somerset Street West housed Irish and Italian immigrants, but today people call it Chinatown because of the prominence of its Chinese restaurants. It is an evolving area: businesses sit in new malls of glass and steel, as well as in converted houses where former parlours have become storefronts. Mature trees still line the roadside.

Somerset Heights is near the Queensway, an accessible location that helps suburban customers reach Chinatown. On weekends they come to shop, dine and meet friends. Parking and traffic problems arise as they commonly do in Chinatowns across the country. This district also offers Chinese churches and help for non-English speakers, amenities that boost visitor numbers.

Ottawa was never a metropolis, and its Chinese community

reached only 300 before World War II. It was so modest that no clan or district associations were formed. But in the 1990s, Ottawa's Chinese population jumped from 7600 in 1991 to 19,860 in 1996, and then to 27,685 in 2001. It became Canada's fifth-largest Chinese settlement.

### Early Settlement

Ottawa's early Chinese settlers worked in the same industries as their compatriots across Canada. The first Chinese who reached the city in the late 1880s was surnamed Tam and he was soon followed by kinsmen sharing that name, also spelled Hum or Hom.[1] They joined 40,000 people in a tough town where lumber was the key industry, even though Ottawa had been the national capital for decades. During the 1900 decade, Chinese numbers increased to 168 when rapid growth of the federal civil service stimulated the rise of laundries and cafés.

Between 1911 and 1921, Chinese-owned restaurants doubled to 16, and the number of laundries peaked during the 1920s at 60. The largest number of wash houses stood along downtown Bank Street (12 in 1909), while other main streets such as Dalhousie, Rideau, Wellington and Somerset had five or six each. Some laundries lasted 40 to 50 years—not often with the same owner because businesses were sold and resold as men returned to China or tried other jobs.

Life was hard. In 1914, just before New Year's Eve, ten Chinese begged for food at the police station; they couldn't support themselves because of the war and their joblessness. They were given 45 kilograms of rice, nine kilograms of beef, four sacks of potatoes and six cabbages.[2] This request was unusual, given the tradition of self-help among the Chinese, but smaller communities had fewer resources.

By 1943 only half of Ottawa's Chinese worked in laundries;[3] the others had switched to restaurants. The eateries,

with names like Boston Café or Capital Lunch, served Western cuisine and employed white waitresses. Even small Chinese communities faced racism, or joined wider protests against it. Ottawa whites agitated against Chinese laundries, alleging that they caused a drop in property values.[4] When a white complainant claimed in 1916 that Chinese laundries and restaurants harboured infectious diseases, the Health Department demanded physical checks of these premises. But the Chinese owners refused to

*Hum Quon, one of the first Chinese in Ottawa, 1893.*

submit and asked the Chinese consul for help. The consul went before Ottawa City Council, which cancelled the action.[5]

Ottawa's Chinese in 1919 formed a benevolent group called the United Chinese Association (UCA).[6] It promptly requested the consul to lobby the federal government on immigration issues.[7] The following year, the Ottawa community followed Toronto's Anti-Restriction Association by starting a local branch to protest the head taxes.[8]

### The China Connection

Chinese groups in Ottawa resembled those in other cities, but their situation was complicated by the national capital factor.

After reformer Liang Qichao visited Parliament in 1903, a branch of his Chinese Empire Reform Association (CERA, later Constitutionalist Party) emerged. After the Republic of China

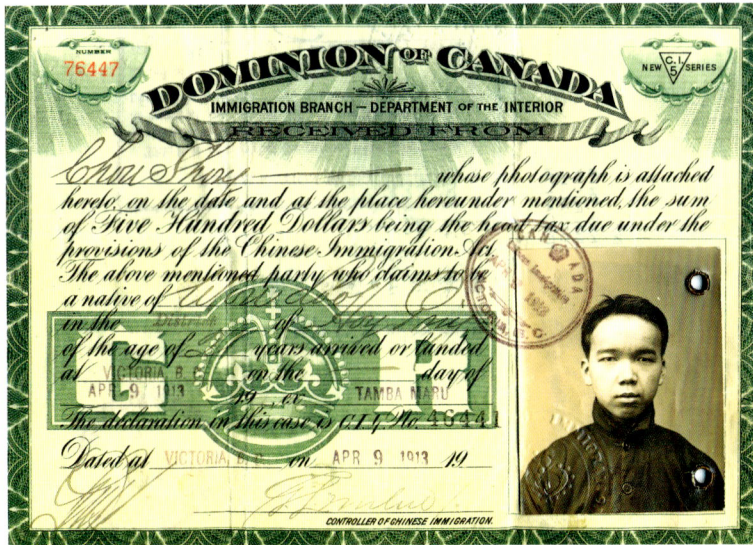

*Certificate showing that Joe (Chow) Shung had paid head tax, 1913.*

was formed, Ottawa's Kuomintang (KMT) attracted 100 members, a hefty portion of Ottawa's Chinese. In response, the smaller numbers of Freemasons and Constitutionalists united against their common foe, the KMT, in a Three Cities United Association there and in Montreal and Toronto in 1928.[9] For several years, the allies jointly celebrated the Chinese New Year in Ottawa with colleagues from the other cities. However, the three groups settled their differences during World War II in order to raise funds for the war effort in China. At the end of the war, representatives from the three cities congregated in Ottawa to celebrate.

Local Chinese leaders took a pro-active role in world affairs, taking advantage of the national capital factor. In 1915 the teacher and students at Ottawa's Chinese school telegrammed the president of China urging him to declare war on Japan.[10]

Four years later, the UCA wrote to the Chinese government to oppose Japan's attempts to dismiss Chinese delegates from the Paris Peace Conference. The UCA also dispatched a supportive note to the delegates.[11] In 1920, at the consul's urging, Ottawa's Chinese formed the Association for Famine Relief in response to a drought in north China.[12] They approached a federal cabinet minister, asking Canada to donate the head taxes collected in 1919 from Chinese immigrants and to ship wheat to China. But the minister refused, claiming that China continued to be a food exporter.[13]

Ottawa also received Chinese dignitaries. China had established a consulate-general in 1908. In 1943, Madam Chiang Kai-shek, the wife of China's generalissimo, addressed Parliament after appearing before the U.S. Congress in Washington. The 1950s and 1960s saw Wong Foon Sien, president of the Vancouver Chinese Benevolent Association, come on annual visits to lobby the federal government on immigration.

## Many Christians

Ottawa's early Chinese community included a few families, many "bachelor" men, a Chinatown, and sympathetic Christian friends. The 1910s saw the arrival of men who would bring their wives and raise Ottawa's first Canadian-born Chinese. These included Joe Sim, Shung Joe, Sue Wong, Shing Wong and James Hum, four of whom raised between six and nine children each.[14]

Shung Joe started his own laundry and worked for ten years before sending for his wife Kai-voon in 1923. She arrived just before the exclusion law. "My mother was lucky," said her son William. "She managed to make it into Canada because she was already on the boat."[15]

Earlier, in 1921, Shung Joe had helped establish the Chinese Mission (later the Chinese United Church), and church members pleaded his wife's case with immigration officials. Kai-voon later became an elder there. William became an entrepreneur in food services, travel and property development. He was also a director of the Chinese Community Association of Ottawa and non-Chinese organizations such as the Ottawa Board of Trade. In 1988 he was appointed to Carleton University's Board of Governors.

In the 1920s Chinatown emerged on Albert Street, between Kent and O'Connor with three laundries, a restaurant and the Wing On grocery store.[16] At this time, most "bachelor" Chinese lived in boarding-houses known as fong-hau. One man recalled:

> 'When I first came to Ottawa, I stayed with my clan brothers for some years. It was very difficult for a Chinese to rent a room at that time. We rented a whole house. There were about ten of us, but people kept moving in and out. All of us paid a share of the rent. Those who were unemployed paid a smaller amount, but would have to do the cooking and the housekeeping. Clan brothers from out-of-town would stay over at our place for the night. There was always a crowd in the house on weekends.'[17]

Christians befriended the Chinese and began offering English classes in 1891. In 1919, 20 Chinese started a YMCA. A year later, the church schools (Presbyterian, Methodist and YMCA) formed the Chinese Mission (later the Chinese United Church), home to Ottawa's first Chinese congregation.[18] Between 1892 and 1922, over 1000 Chinese students passed through church-sponsored English classes.[19]

Ottawa had a high ratio of Chinese Christians: 59 percent in 1931. Only Halifax, with 77 percent, was more fervent. The low numbers of Chinese in these two cities suggest that in smaller centres the Chinese were more likely to join a church community. The Chinese Mission was a busy place. During the 1930s it offered Chinese language classes. It was the place where the young Canadian-born Chinese organized dances, fashion shows, fundraisers and sports.[20] They even formed an ice hockey team called the Aces, which toured the region and played exhibition games to raise funds for war relief. In response, a Chinese hockey team emerged in Montreal too.

*The Chinese consulate, where Chinese sought help, 1913.*

The Albert Street China-town grew to contain four restaurants, three laundries, two groceries, and three other shops. Several Chinese social clubs were gambling houses that provided jobs and shelter to jobless Chinese during the Depression. However, Chinese numbers shrank by a tenth during that decade.

## The Cold War

Ottawa's Chinese population grew quickly after World War II, soon increasing by a quarter. Many of Ottawa's Chinese had obtained Canadian citizenship and could quickly submit sponsorship applications. In the 1950s, the Chinese number topped 1000 as wives and offspring joined husbands and fathers here.

The Chinese United Church became the biggest and most influential Chinese organization; prior to 1982, most large-

*Chinese Freemasons celebrating VJ Day, 1945.*

scale community events occurred there. For young newcomers who worked mostly in the restaurant trade, the church sponsored English classes, a Chinese newspaper reading room, table tennis and basketball. When these young men married and had children, the congregation grew even more, and the church held classes for children and for adults.[21]

It was in the 1950s that Jimmy Kwan sent for his son Alan from Hong Kong. They both worked as waiters in William Joe's Cathay Restaurant (on Albert Street). In 1971 Alan opened the Shanghai Restaurant on Somerset Street, one of the first Chinese businesses in what would become today's Chinatown. Pierre Trudeau often ate at the Shanghai, which passed into the hands of Alan's children in the 2000s.

The 1950s also saw other changes. Foreign students attended the region's universities and in 1955 Hong Kong students formed the Ottawa Chinese Catholic Community. Three years later, the Chinese Community Centre of Ottawa (CCCO) succeeded the earlier benevolent group and became embroiled in the two-China issue partly because the national capital hosted diplomats and trade missions.

Thirty Ottawa Chinese wrote to Canada's prime minister in 1968, opposing recognition of Mainland China. Later that year, after Trudeau's election, other Chinese groups came to Ottawa to lobby for the same cause. One organization went as far as to claim that an exchange of embassies with Beijing "would fling the door wide open to a flood of Communist agents to this continent. A Chinese Communist embassy in Ottawa would become the field headquarters and commanding post to direct the guerilla warfare in North America."[22]

Later, the two-China conflict affected the CCCO executive. In the elections of 1970 and 1976, so-called pro-China candidates were accused of trying to seize control of the organization during board elections. But most community members maintained a neutrality. "When a person becomes a Canadian citizen, he should not be involved in the politics of his Old Country. ... I don't think we can gain anything by this 'left-right' rivalry."[23]

Others had residual Cold War fears: "I am afraid to join any 'leftist' or 'rightist' Chinese association. I have a good job, and I don't want the RCMP to investigate my activities. Some of these Chinese organizations may be involved in subversive activities."[24]

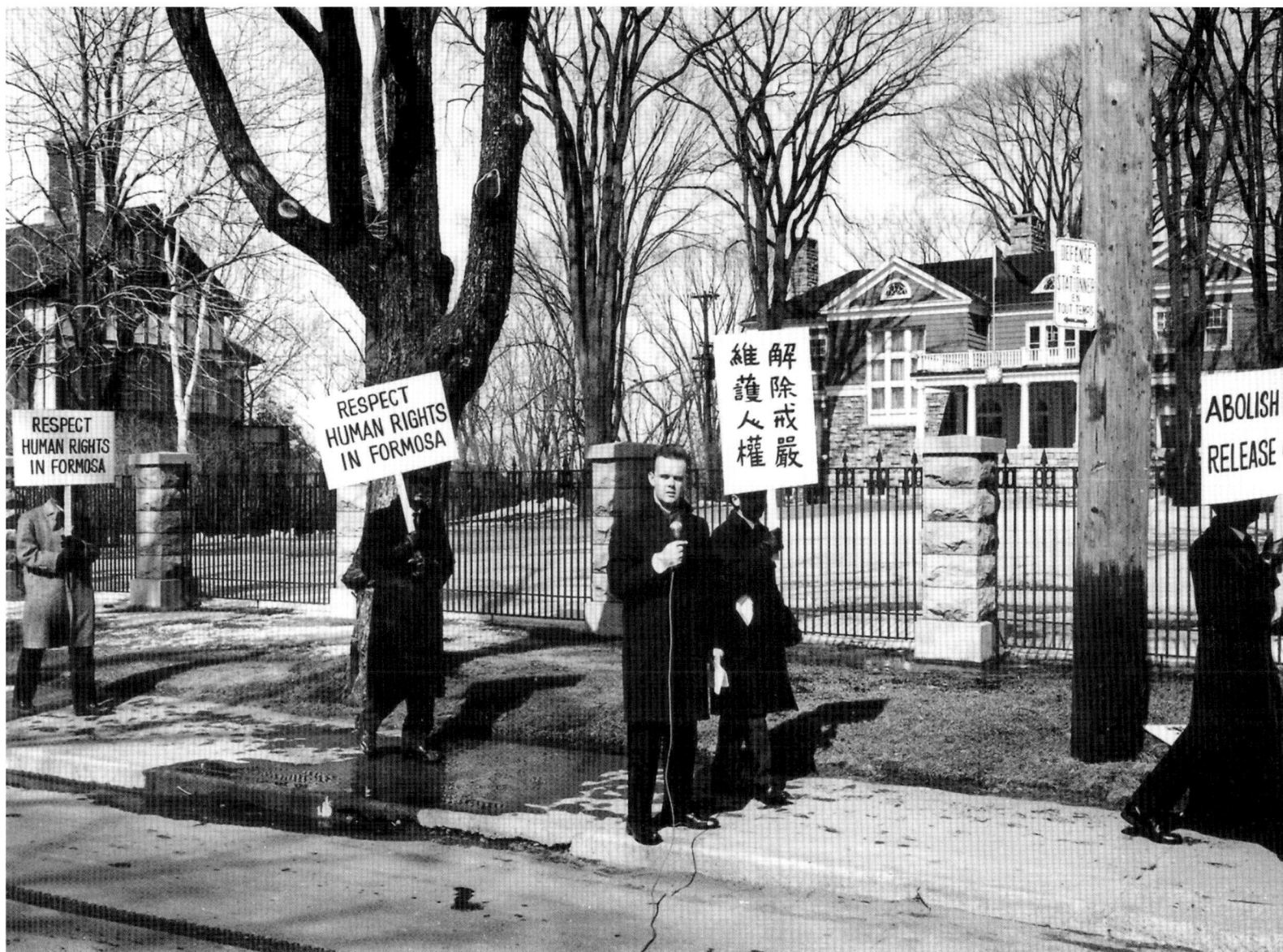

*Protesting against martial law at the Chinese (Taiwan) Embassy, 1965.*

*Alan Kwan and his father Jimmy were waiters before starting the Shanghai Restaurant on Somerset Street, c1971.*

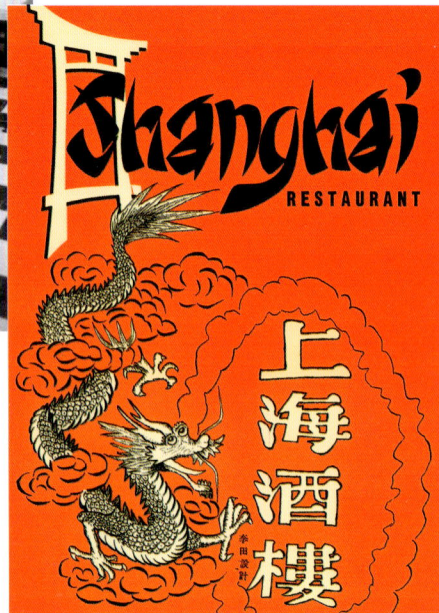

## Mandarin Dominates

Chinese firms sprang up on Somerset Street West in the 1970s as Ottawa's Chinese population doubled from 3600 to 8200 thanks to immigration from Hong Kong. The community also grew from Indochinese refugees. In 1979 the city of Ottawa spearheaded Project 4000, in which 360 local church and community groups sponsored 3800 Boat People refugees. They arrived just as the 1982–83 recession struck, and suffered jobless rates that were three times higher than other Canadians. And over 500 Centretown residents signed a petition against the newcomers, fearing their presence would cause a drop in property values.

In time the refugees integrated into the mainstream, but it took hard work. Lan Eng Yeh came from Vietnam in 1982, where he had been a mathematics teacher. In Ottawa, he cleaned full-time at nights, bell-hopped on weekends, and did lunchtime monitoring at a local school. He wasn't able to get further education because he had three children to care for. "My hope now is for the next generation," he said. "I can't complain, that's life."[25]

In the early 1980s, City Council helped redevelop the Somerset Street area. More businesses arose, including Humphrey Plaza, built in 1982. That year also, the CCCO built the 12-storey complex that held 46 apartment units, a community hall, a library and the headquarters for the organization, but it was located elsewhere. By 1986, a quarter of the residents of Dalhousie North were from China or Southeast Asia.[26]

That same year, Chinese commercial groups wanted to shape the area into a more distinctive Chinatown to draw more business. Other merchants and area residents wanted Somerset Street to remain multicultural and not to highlight one race. They preferred a variety of shops and restaurants, and argued that new businesses shouldn't push out existing ones. But those who favoured a distinctive Chinatown, including the mayor, feared that a more inclusive approach would make the street "just another commercial business strip." After many consultations, plans for a distinctive Chinatown were dropped, and Somerset Street developed on its own. But people continued to use the term "Chinatown" for Somerset Street, and this area became a focal point for Ottawa's Chinese even when most of them did not live nearby. For a while, six of Ottawa's nine Chinese churches were in or near Chinatown, where its members shopped and socialized after services.[27]

Hong Kong immigrants from this period left a lasting imprint on Ottawa. Organizations of the 1970s included the National Capital Chinese Community Newsletter. The Ontario Chinese Association recognized the Mainland and not Taiwan as the government of China and introduced the new China's culture to Chinese Canadians. And the Ottawa Chinese Community Service Centre provided many settlement services, including counselling and language training. Artist Bing-lin Wong worked at Environment Canada and the Canadian Museum of Civilization and designed their logos. He did the same for Gloucester Hydro, the Chinese Canadian National Council, and Chinese Canadian Community TV.

By 1989 a third of Ottawa's Chinese were from Hong Kong. Some had arrived during the late 1960s as students, while others came in the mid-1980s in advance of Hong Kong's handover to China in 1997. Some offshore money was attracted in the late 1980s, though much less than that destined for Vancouver and Toronto. Ottawa was viewed as a secondary market, slower but safer, where Hong Kong investors purchased shopping plazas, strip malls, and secondary manufacturing facilities.[28] Finally, the Ottawa chapter of the Hong Kong-Canada Business Association brought the dragon boat races to Ottawa in 1993. By 2001 these races had grown from a 25-team event to one involving 168 teams.

Hong Kong Chinese established the Ottawa Chinese Alliance Church in 1973 and St. Peter's Chinese Church (Anglican) in 1980 as well as providing new blood to the Chinese Catholic Community of 1955. The latter two churches benefited from newcomers who had been Christians prior to immigration, while those who became Christians after landing here tended to attend newer denominations. From 1990 on, the Ottawa Chinese Alliance Church became the largest Chinese religious organization, and it opened three more churches.

In the 1990s newcomers from Mainland China were the most numerous, and they changed the community in various ways. Mandarin became the dominant language rather than Cantonese, such that the Chinese United Church shifted from English-Cantonese to English-Mandarin services in 2001. While many Hong Kong immigrants had commercial and business backgrounds, many Mainland Chinese had high education levels (doctors, engineers, scholars). They also came for Ottawa's high-tech industry. Later, the crash in this sector led to the formation of the Sino-Canadian Hi-Tech Exchange Association, a networking group. It attracted over 1100 members, some of whom returned to China for career opportunities there.[29] Others undertook enterprising attempts to advance business ventures between China and Canada.

*Vivienne Poy, first Chinese Canadian appointed to Canada's Senate, 1998.*

Mainland Chinese started a weekly newspaper, *Canada China News*, and saw its circulation rise from 1000 to 10,000. They formed the Ottawa Mandarin Alliance Church, and began hosting Chinese New Year celebrations at the Ottawa Congress Centre. They started cultural organizations to teach Mandarin and other aspects of Chinese culture to Canadians. Recognizing that

Mandarin-speaking seniors were left out of Cantonese-language programs and often confined to their homes, the Chinese Cultural Centre of Ottawa organized activities to help them function independently in a new English-speaking environment.

## The National Stage

The national capital provided the Chinese communities with public venues for expressing public opinions. Some issues reminded Mainland immigrants why they had left their homeland; other issues provoked solidarity with China or other overseas Chinese.

In June 1989, after the Tiananmen Square incident shocked the world, protesters from Montreal, Kingston and Quebec City rallied in Ottawa at the Chinese embassy. They burned an effigy of the Chinese premier. People wept openly. After a moment of silence was observed, about a thousand protestors marched to the Peace Tower.[30]

When China's president visited Ottawa in 1997, Tibetan groups protested against China's occupation of their homeland, while Taiwanese groups expressed dismay at Canada's belief that increased trade with China would improve human rights there.

In 1998, 500 Chinese Canadians demonstrated outside the Indonesian embassy, highlighting the ethnic violence that targeted the Chinese minority there. Mobs had rampaged for three days through Indonesian cities, burning Chinese shops, killing Chinese residents and raping Chinese women.

The following year, 350 demonstrators marched to the American Embassy to denounce NATO's bombing of the Chinese Embassy in Belgrade. One angry protester pointed out, "If you have the best of everything, the best airforce, the best technology, then why can you make mistakes?"[31]

In 2002 Falun Gong members won an exemption from the city, allowing them to continue hanging banners across the street from the Chinese embassy. Since May 2001, they had held vigils there calling for China to stop persecuting co-practitioners.

One other legacy of the Hong Kong Chinese was the local chapter of the Chinese Canadian National Council, formed in response to the nation-wide protest against the W5 TV program "Campus Giveaway." The Ottawa chapter had immigrant and Canadian-born members, and was active for several decades. It spoke out on issues concerning mass media stereotypes, racism, multiculturalism and immigration, and also promoted Chinese-Canadian arts and culture.

By the turn of the century, "Chinese" (Cantonese and Mandarin) had become Ottawa's top non-official mother tongue. But the Chinese were not the largest racial minority; the African-Canadians, at 35,000, held that spot.

*Chinatown, late 1990s.*

98

# 7

# MONTREAL: BILINGUAL AND TRILINGUAL

For Saint Jean Baptiste Day 2004, the Vietnamese Chinese Association of Montreal organized a day-long celebration in Chinatown. At the start of festivities, hosts released blue and white (Quebec's colours) balloons that lifted the province's flag high into the sky. In his opening remarks, the association president recalled how the Vietnamese Chinese had arrived in Quebec as refugees 25 years before, and how a million of their compatriots had perished while fleeing Communism. He thanked the Quebec government for its wel-

*One of four gates to Montreal's Chinatown, 2004.*

come and assistance. Speeches were given in French and Cantonese. The variety show that followed included Chinese music and martial arts as well as Québécois music and folk dancing. These details highlight the diversity of the members of Canada's Chinese communities as well as their keen desire to integrate into their new home societies.

Of all of Canada's Chinatowns, Montreal's has the most Chinese gates: four, one in each direction. It also features the most public art. Dr. Sun Yat-sen

## LA TAXE DES CHINOIS

**IL LEUR EN COUTE MAINTENANT $500 AU LIEU DE $50 POUR ENTRER DANS NOTRE PAYS.**

Depuis que la nouvelle taxe imposable pour l'entrée des Chinois sur le sol canadien est mise en vigueur l'immigration a cessé. Cette taxe qui était autrefois de $50 est maintenant fixée à $500, ce qui demande chez les émigrants, une petite fortune qui pourrait les faire vire relativement à l'aise dans leur quand ie décompte est fait de la taxe, des frais de voyage, etc., on arrive à bien près de $1,000.

Lee Chu le chef de la colonie chinoise à Montréal, questionné au sujet de la taxe nouvelle, nous a assuré que le droit d'entrée aurait pour effet de faire cesser l'émigration chinoise sur le Canada.

Lee Chu, nous a donné ansi la traduction du message envoyé en Chine, aux agences d'émigration. Ce message se lit comme suit :

A nos frères de Chine,

Vous êtes par les présentes avertis que vous aurez à payer $500 pour entrer sur le sol canadien.

LEE CHU.

Les Chinois, devant l'implacabilité de la taxe, cessent d'écrire à leurs parents en Chine ; sur les faire venir au Canada. Ainsi, Montréal, qui devait s'enrichir de deux ou trois cents nouveaux fils du Ciel pendant le cours de l'année, va échapper à l'invasion.

Place shows an elegant façade of Chinese doors, columns and roof decorations, along with a stone mural of a landscape. St. Urbain Street has two Chinese murals: one of graceful musicians and the other of figures from the classic Journey from the West. Raw stone sculptures have been placed on the roads and the new Chinese hospital boasts interior and exterior art installations.

Summer finds Chinatown at its liveliest as vendors, tourists and locals fill the street, especially on Promenade de la Gauchetière, a pedestrian mall paved with brick and stone. Cantonese, Mandarin, Toisanese, French and English are all heard. This Chinatown is a bit European: the side streets are narrow and some older limestone buildings are topped with steep Mansard-like roofs. The district is full of shops, restaurants and service groups at the hub of a Chinese community that is dispersed across the region. The area will continue to evolve in line with the 1996 Chinatown Development Plan, which will expand Chinatown, improve links to surrounding areas, consolidate the commercial core, and improve its housing and quality of life.

### An Ancient City

Montreal, Canada's second-oldest city was founded in 1535, and was long the nation's commercial centre. Chinese arrived here singly, as servants, well before ongoing Asian immigration on the west coast. One Chinese lived in the Saint Joseph district in 1825.[1] Four decades later, a few Chinese attended Saint Laurent School. It wasn't until 1877 that Jos Song Long's laundry opened on Craig Street (now Saint Antoine). Seven Chinese appeared in the 1881 census, but an 1880 newspaper mentioned thirty.[2] They had likely travelled from the United States or across the Atlantic, because the CPR was still unfinished.

The Chinese arrived just as Montreal was entering the industrial age, and their numbers expanded with the growing city. Factories emerged and the city tripled to half a million residents between 1881 and 1911. By 1901 Montreal had Canada's third-largest Chinese community (900 members). Their hand laundries spread across the city and formed the biggest such industry in the country.

Other Chinese businesses also appeared. On Notre Dame

*Above: Advertisement explaining head tax increase, 1904.*
*Below: Chinatown emerged in an old part of Montreal, 1908.*

Street, Wong Kee sold Asian spices, teas, dishes and fabrics to whites. In 1891 Jung Fook and Wong Wing opened a similar store on Lagauchetière Street (later Chinatown).[3] Merchants imported groceries and supplied Chinese throughout Quebec and the Maritimes via Montreal's railway connections.

Laundries featured stiff competition, long hours and low returns. Between 1894 and 1911, Chinese opened 1063 washhouses in the city, but only a quarter of them survived.[4] The first were north of Old Montreal in Saint Laurent, a commercial area of low rents. Wash houses spread to other working-class districts: Saint Louis, Sainte Marie, and then Saint Jean Baptiste.[5] But dispersal didn't guarantee success, because of competition from local women who took laundry home to wash.

There were also other institutional challenges. In the 1890s a hand laundry licence cost $50, much more than the five to eight dollars charged greengrocers, bakers or milk sellers. Chinese couldn't afford it or refused to pay. As for business taxes, over 100 Chinese were fined for non-payment in 1896 and 1897. Luckily, their lawyer found a flaw in the law that cancelled penalties totalling $4000. But ten Chinese were jailed in 1900. Believing themselves harassed and unfairly taxed, the Chinese petitioned the city at large, demanding an exemption. This proved fruitless, and 146 men were fined. Their resistance lasted another year before collapsing.[6]

When Montreal's economy cooled down in 1913, hand laundries lost business. In 1914 white owners of mechanized laundries stirred up reaction against Chinese laundrymen. In response, the Chinese Benevolent Society (CBS) was founded. At that time, a laundry worker earned six to eight dollars a week, plus room and board.[7] The following year, white laundry owners launched a newspaper campaign further attacking Chinese laundries and calling for a boycott. The province then

*One of many wash houses in the city, c1915.*

levied a $50 tax on Chinese laundrymen, on top of the $50 license fee. The CBS advised them not to pay, hired a lawyer and sought help from the Chinese consul and the Archbishop of Montreal.[8] These efforts were futile.

The Chinese also worked as servants, tobacconists, barbers, and tailors. Cafés attracted operators, but success was uneven: of 29 eateries begun from 1900 to 1910, only eight lasted longer than five years. By 1921 Chinese-run restaurants and cafés numbered 55 and they became more popular until the Depression.

**The Three Clans**

Montreal's early Chinese came mostly from three clans: Lee, Wong, and Hom (also known as Taam). The Lees formed a group in 1898 and claimed 100 members in 1905. One leader was Lee Chu, a merchant and official court interpreter with extensive connections: at his son's birth, non-Chinese police officials, judges and a lawyer visited his home, and the daily press mentioned the event.[9] (There was also a Chinese policeman surnamed Lee, but foes put a $500 price tag on his head.[10])

The Wongs organized their first group in 1903. The fact that Lee Chu's successor as court interpreter was a Wong confirmed clan rivalries. For example, a laundryman facing competition or feeling cheated by other clans would complain to his surname group.[11]

Chinatown was in Dufferin, a district of light industries and a mixed English, Irish and French population. By 1897 there were six Chinese stores on Lagauchetière Street between Saint Urbain and Clark. Chinese workers picked up their mail at these stores, which were allied to clans and sometimes were the headquarters of clan groups. These merchants began buying nearby commercial properties.

The merchants quickly adopted Western ways. In 1894 reporter Edith Eaton (whose Chinese mother lived in Montreal) recorded her visit to hotel keeper Wing Sing's home:

> *It was an ordinarily furnished apartment, very much in appearance like the living room of a European family in moderate circumstances, the only difference being that the walls were hung from top to bottom with long bamboo panels covered with paper, on which were printed Chinese characters, signifying good luck. A sewing machine was visible and in use, a proof that the Chinese do march forward in the van of civilization. Mrs. Wing Sing is quite an expert operator.*[12]

She was also one of only three Chinese women in Montreal. By 1911 that number rose to 33, and soon Canadian-born Chinese children appeared in Chinatown.

The politics of modernizing China were at hand. Merchants favoured the Chinese Empire Reform Association (CERA) and established a Montreal branch in 1903. The Chinese Freemasons also emerged that year, and later raised $4000 for Dr. Sun Yat-sen's revolution.

By 1917 Chinatown contained five restaurants, ten stores, five rooming houses and at least ten Chinese associations, clubs and missions. Most Chinese lived at laundries spread across the city. New clan groups were formed, and they battled over illegal gambling in 1922.[13] In 1926 jobless Chinese were charged with vagrancy, and Chinatown associations asked the Chinese consul to intervene. Other ties with the homeland involved raising money for a high school in Tai-shan county, public mourning for Dr. Sun Yat-sen's death, and Chinese McGill University students' publishing a booklet in English about Japanese imperialism.

In December 1933 Freemasons and KMT (Chinese Nationalist Party) members brawled in Chinatown. Forty-five people wielded Chinese swords, clubs and knives. Windows were smashed and chairs flew through the air. In fifteen minutes, six men lay unconscious. The police arrested 25 suspects. The Freemasons claimed a recent parade had made their opponents envious. Another observer told newspaper readers that the dispute was nothing more than a disagreement among gambling factions that did not involve the ordinary Chinese.[14]

## Catholics and Protestants

Christians helped the Chinese, but in Montreal the immigrants faced a choice between Protestant and Catholic churches. Protestants from Emmanuel Congregational Church first organized a Sunday school for Chinese in 1884. A decade later, over 160 Chinese were studying English at 10 churches. Chan Nam-sing and Joseph Thompson, missionaries from China, started the Chinese Presbyterian Mission in 1897.

Reverend Chan's son recalled:

> My father was six foot three, a huge man by our standards. In the old days a lot of the immigrants were badly educated people who had enough difficulty just being better Buddhists. My father was taunted a lot at first. He used to carry the sick to hospitals because no one could afford a buggy. And he protected them when Canadians jeered at their pigtails and costumes. As a man who spoke English, he helped them cope with different laws and habits.[15]

In Montreal, the Catholic Church was powerful. While it and the Protestants both gave financial help, language classes, children's education and translation services to the Chinese, each church had different advantages.

The Protestants provided the Chinese with a pastor of their own kind, Chan Nam-sing, who stayed until 1920. They allowed non-Christian Chinese to be buried in their part of Mount Royal Cemetery. And they did not pressure the Chinese to abandon traditional practices such as ancestor worship (which Catholics viewed as pagan). For example, Reverend Chan kept the Chinese calendar and celebrated Chinese New Year. At his son's birth in 1904, he wore Chinese dress to receive guests, and reportedly wished the infant: "May your ashes one day rest in your homeland under the care of Confucius." The newborn's Chinese full-month ceremony occurred before his church baptism.[16]

As for the Catholic Church, when it started language classes for the Chinese in 1901 both English and French were taught. French was useful for Chinese laundrymen who saw French-speaking Montrealers daily. In 1916 a sisterhood of

*Montrealers liked to eat, dance and drink in Chinatown, 1930.*

nuns opened an elementary school for Chinese children, fully supported by the Catholic School Commission. Most important, Catholics were key players in the Montreal Chinese Hospital.

During the 1918 influenza epidemic, 3000 people died in Montreal. Nuns set up a ten-bed hospital near Chinatown to

*Chinatown stores were gathering places for the community, 1940.*

help the Chinese. As one old-timer recalled:

> *Chinatown was just like a dead town then. All stores were closed. Everybody stayed home. If we really needed to get something from outside, we got to wear a mask. Wong-Lo-Gup was the only herbal medicine available for us, all laundry shops were full of these 'life-savers.' However it did work.*[17]

When the epidemic ended, Chinese merchants raised $2000 for a down payment on a hospital building. Sisters of the Immaculate Conception provided administration, and three part-time francophone doctors were on hand. The Chinese

Catholic Mission was founded nearby in 1922. Between 1920 and 1950, over 500 Chinese adults converted to Catholicism.

Fifty Chinese families lived in Montreal in the 1930s. The Protestants offered Canadian-born Chinese a kindergarten, a band, a Canadian Girls in Training group, a Chinese school, and a Young People's Society. The Catholic mission had a kindergarten, a youth club, a Boy Scout troop, a summer camp and a choir. The Canadian-born Chinese were mostly English-speaking because their parents had come from British Columbia or south China, where Protestant missionaries were active. In Montreal, many merchants joined the Chinese Presbyterian Mission.

But not all families had well-to-do merchant backgrounds. Cooks, waiters and laundrymen took up with French-Canadian women, and grocers and restaurateurs married such women, usually as second wives.[18]

## Wing and Wong Wing

The Canadian-born generation had been prominent among 40 Chinese Montrealers who enlisted in the Canadian Armed Forces during World War II. On the home front, the Chinese set up a Chinatown Security Brigade (Bao-An) to protect property and civilians. They did military drills, firearms testing and first aid training, and they raised over $400,000 for war relief in China.

After the war, families started modern businesses. Arthur Lee's Wing Noodles Limited began making fortune cookies, noodles, and wonton skins in 1946. Lee had been born in Montreal but went to Hong Kong in 1935. When the Japanese invaded, he escaped to China and walked 150 miles to his ancestral village. For the next four years, he lived as his forefathers had, working in the fields. Fortunately, the Japanese did not occupy that area until towards the end of the war,[19] and Lee was able to return to Canada in 1946.

The adult children of Ham Wong started Wong Wing Food Products in 1947, producing frozen spring rolls, fried rice and other entrées. Its factory in Chinatown had 110 employees in 1970.[20] It became Canada's largest supplier of such foods in the 1990s, and was bought by the giant McCain's Food Limited in 2002. Director Pauline Wong liked the fact that McCain's was also a family-run firm with similar customers and similar suppliers.[21]

Wong's father had come to Canada in 1908. He married a French-Canadian woman and they struggled to raise eight children. The family was poor, and the children recalled asking the parish priest for shoes and collecting vegetables that had fallen off delivery trucks. One of Wong's brothers, Raymond, became head of the company and was active in the Chinese community even though he did not speak or read Chinese. He helped organize the Chinese Service Association, which opened a language school in 1956. English and French were taught to parents and children, and Chinese was available to children between the ages of four and ten. Later, Raymond Wong worked on the Chinatown Caisse Populaire (credit union), the Chinese United Centre, and the Chinese Hospital. He also supported schools and orphanages in China. In 1994, Concordia University awarded him an Award of Distinction to honour his business acumen and community work.

**Body Without a Heart**

The arrival of residents' wives and offspring after 1947 helped restore the dwindling population. Young newcomers formed the East Wind Club and published a newsletter with local and international news. On weekends, Chinese from throughout the city congregated in Chinatown. But their increased numbers couldn't save Chinatown from bulldozers.

By the 1960s only 600 of Montreal's 8000 Chinese lived in Chinatown. In 1963 the Canadian Broadcasting Corporation

*VJ Day celebrations in Chinatown, 1945.*

eyed this convenient downtown location for its headquarter site. But local merchants drew up their own plans for redevelopment. The city sided with the Chinese and the CBC went elsewhere. However, the merchants' plans were shelved in 1968 because of indifference from Chinatown's older, conservative factions.[22]

Then Chinatown began shrinking. The widening of Dorchester Street (later René Lévesque Boulevard) destroyed housing. The Chinese Hospital was closed for health and safety reasons in 1962, and reopened three years later away from Chinatown. New construction blocked further growth. On two sides ran the high-speed René Lévesque Boulevard and Ville

*The Nanking Restaurant's prominent sign glittered all night, 1974.*

Marie Tunnel of the Trans-Canada Highway. In 1962, in preparation for new Hydro Quebec offices, the Chinese United Church was bulldozed and many residents were relocated. The Complexe Desjardins project then helped freeze Chinatown's northwest boundary.

By 1970 a national conference in Calgary had called for a stop to the destruction of Canadian Chinatowns by government-led "urban renewal" impulses. Subsequently, city planners in cities such as Toronto, Vancouver and Calgary invited community input. In Montreal, however, governments paid little heed to Chinese Canadians. For example, in 1972 the federal government launched the massive Guy Favreau project, a multi-towered office-apartment complex, in Chinatown. Chinatown landowners protested: Marcel Wong of Wong Wing Food Products said it would cut out the spiritual and cultural centre of the community, and leave the people with a body without a heart.[23]

Although the mayor vowed the city had no plan for any development that might adversely affect Chinatown, expropriation proceeded.[24] It ate up six acres of Chinatown, including two churches, the Wong Wing Food Products factory, and other dwellings. Only the Chinese Catholic Church, a designated historic building, was saved. Protests from Chinese and groups such as Save Montreal led to community consultations in 1977. But while they proceeded, demolition continued.[25] In the end, the only result of the protests was that the scale of the project, completed in 1983, was reduced.

In 1981 the city widened Saint Urbain Street for increased traffic from nearby public buildings. Chinese community protests saved the Lee family building from demolition, but the widening proceeded and the Pagoda Park landmark was removed (without telling the Chinese). Ironically, the pagoda, donated by Arthur Lee of Wing Noodles, had been "dedicated to the cause of peace and harmony among all Canadians." One observer remarked, "I think that pagoda is symbolic of how the city deals with the Chinese community. These people come in and destroy it, break it into pieces, then they bring it back if they want."[26]

The Montreal Convention Centre, completed in 1983, swallowed a block of properties and blocked growth toward the south. In 1984 the city zoned most of Lagauchetiere Street east of Saint Laurent Street as residential. This stopped businesses from expanding eastward, the only opening. One enraged businessman slammed city officials who presumed to know Chinatown by lunching at local restaurants. "They say, 'How's business, Chow Lee?' but the Chinese will never say 'Business good.' So Chow Lee says, 'Oh, business very bad, very bad, too much competition' and this guy from the city thinks he's going to be Santa Claus. He'll take care of Chow Lee by making sure no more restaurants are built in Chinatown."[27]

Despite angry community protests, the city made only a small concession. Unfortunately, this issue occurred during high emigration from Hong Kong and caused investors from the colony to avoid Montreal.[28]

**Newcomers in New Quebec**

Meanwhile, the numbers of Montreal's Chinese had risen to over 10,000 by 1971 and kept growing. Many newcomers were sponsored by relatives; others were professionals and skilled workers who came independently. As well, 7000 refugees from Vietnam, Cambodia and Laos arrived in 1979–80, some speaking French because France had colonized their homelands.

Most post-1967 immigrants were from Hong Kong. They, along with students at Montreal's post-secondary schools, launched several key groups. The Chinese Family Services of

*The Hong Kong Tailors on la Gauchetiere Street, 1981.*

Greater Montreal was founded in 1976 to assist elderly Chinese and then Sino-Vietnamese refugees. The Chinese Neighbourhood Society emerged three years later to offer settlement services and cultural events to local residents. Newcomers also started Chinese-language radio broadcasting (1969), TV broadcasting (1971) and newspapers such as *Wah Sing Bao*, the Chinese Press, and Chinada News.

The 1960s saw Québécois nationalism flourish. Over the years, this created problems for immigrants, especially English-

*Redevelopment of Chinatown, 1981.*

speakers. Some newcomers from Hong Kong found it romantic to try to learn a new language. But those who found it inconvenient and threatening left Montreal for other Canadian cities.[29]

Two years after the province designated French as Quebec's official language, the Parti Québécois took power. It felt Canada let too many anglophone and allophone immigrants into Quebec, so it halted English classes for them,[30] and forced their children to attend French-language schools. About a thousand Chinese families left Montreal between 1975 and 1977.[31] Many anglophone families and businesses also left.

But Quebeckers weren't ready to abandon Canada: 60 percent voted No in the 1980 referendum on separation. Still, their ties with Canada were unstable as attempts to recognize Quebec as a distinct society failed (Meech Lake Accord 1990 and Charlottetown Accord 1992). As well, the province reaffirmed its French-language priorities by using the Charter's "notwithstanding clause" to override a 1988 Supreme Court ruling on Quebec's language law.

The political uncertainty led to economic instability and stagnation as investors steered clear of the province. However, the province used immigration to address its financial issues.

After the category for Entrepreneur immigrants was set up in 1984, Quebec pursued these immigrants by opening an office in Hong Kong. Provincial officials boasted they had the cheapest hydro, land and rents in North America.[32] Realtors claimed Quebec investors could earn a return two to four percent higher than in Ontario or British Columbia.[33] A flurry of Quebec-bound visas resulted, partly because entry requirements were looser: entrepreneurs were not required to submit a specific project.

Some immigrants bridged the needle trades of Hong Kong and Montreal. Entrepreneurs in the garment industry found that Montreal was stronger than Toronto in this regard, and that many people involved in Montreal's garment industry spoke English.[34] When a category for Investor immigrants was created in 1986, Quebec attracted much Asian capital because funds went through registered brokers. In other provinces, the absence of this requirement caused the loss or mismanagement of immigrant funds.

In the next ten years, Quebec took in almost 15,000 business immigrants from China, Hong Kong and Taiwan. They invested $871 million and created 9,000 jobs. From Hong Kong alone, 4,295 immigrants pumped nearly $200 million into Quebec.[35] Other overseas investors turned to Montreal because real estate was too costly in Vancouver and Toronto.

Immigrants looked elsewhere, usually Toronto and Vancouver, before moving to Montreal. Those who came to Montreal liked the lower real estate costs and the smaller Chinese community, factors which provided a better chance of business success.[36]

Other immigrants who landed in Montreal didn't stay, heading instead to Toronto or Vancouver. The language requirements of Quebec were daunting to some. Many tried to learn French, and some could get by without learning French depending on where they lived. But everyone knew that overall advancement was limited for those who spoke no French.[37]

### To Stay or Go

From the mid-1980s on, many Hong Kong and Taiwan immigrants settled in Brossard, on the south shore of the St. Lawrence. It offered reasonable prices for large lots and new houses, and quick access to Montreal's Chinatown. By 1994 over 6000 Chinese lived there. After 1994, when immigration from Hong Kong dropped, business in Chinatown and Brossard slowed down for a short time. "Our community is shrinking," said Anthony Wong, vice-president of the Montreal Chinatown Chamber of Commerce. "We are losing the immigrants. They don't stay here. And we are also losing our young people. They find the job market easier in Toronto."[38]

One stable element of the community was the elderly, who had boosted Chinatown's Chinese population to 1500 in 1996 thanks to new senior citizens' housing. Chinatown had 150 businesses and 3000 children enrolled in Chinese language schools. By the new millennium, immigration from mainland China helped Brossard boom again and its Taschereau Boulevard became known as Chinatown South. Social workers found that immigrants from China planned to stay in Quebec, unlike some immigrants from Hong Kong who hoped to return to their home-land.[39] Many of these immigrants from China were highly educated, experienced in technical work, and familiar with globalization. Such entrepreneurs were keen to do business with China.[40]

### Challenging the Law

In 1987, when language inspectors threatened Chinatown businesses, 17 Chinese groups formed a coalition. The inspectors demanded that French words be twice as prominent as Chinese words on signs, but the coalition wanted existing signs kept. Chinese Quebeckers accepted the French Language Charter as an affirmative action program designed to affirm the well-being and linguistic survival of French Canadians.[41] One coalition member noted that Montreal's Chinatown was more French than Toronto's Chinatown was English,[42] while another leader resented having to change after a century of living in Quebec.[43]

Nor did Quebec nationalists approve of the inspectors' action. The Société St. Jean Baptiste noted that it was English rather than Chinese that posed a threat to French. Eventually a compromise was struck: inspectors would ease up on the signs if Chinese restaurants worked harder at putting French on menus. As well, the government agreed to study the question of what language should be on trademark signs in Chinatown.[44]

In the 1995 referendum, Chinese-speakers canvassed Chinatown to get people onto the voters' list. By then, allophones (people whose mother tongue was neither French nor English) formed 11 percent of Montreal's population. Historically, allophones were allied with Quebec's English-speaking communities, but they also had feelings for Quebec. A trilingual lawyer of Chinese descent said: "We feel that we're Quebeckers—no doubt about it. But we feel we're just as much Canadians as we are Quebeckers—and just as much Chinese as we are Canadians or Quebeckers."

He also noted that young Chinese Montrealers, especially those from Vietnam and Cambodia, were integrating into francophone life but still faced discrimination and difficulty finding work.[45] When the referendum was narrowly defeated, the premier blamed "money and the ethnic vote" for thwarting the wishes of francophones.

The Montreal Chinese Hospital took Quebec's Office de la Langue Française to court in 1998, when the Office ruled that two nursing positions needed only a working knowledge of Chinese. The hospital wanted nurses who were *fluent* in Chinese. A court ruled in favour of the hospital and thankfully the government did not appeal.

### Francophone Future?

In 2001 Toronto and Vancouver's two largest visible minorities were Chinese and South Asians. In Montreal, Chinese ranked fifth after African-Canadians, Arabs/West Asians, South Asians and Latin Americans. The Chinese rank may rise, given that Montreal overtook Vancouver as the second most popular

destination of immigrants in 2002. Between 1991 and 2001, 14,000 newcomers from China formed the second largest group of immigrants destined for Montreal.

The test in Quebec, as elsewhere in Canada, is whether the province's Declaration on Ethnic and Race Relations will hold true. It seeks to encourage "every person to fully take part in Quebec's economic, social and cultural development, regardless of that person's race, colour, religion, ethnic or national origin."

*Sign says "Sidewalk Sale organized by Chinese Chamber of Commerce, 2004."*

# *8*

# HALIFAX: FROM SEA TO SHINING SEA

The Chinese have never been Halifax's largest racial minority; that honour belongs to the older African-Canadian community. Nor did the Halifax Chinese work in direct competition with white workers. What's more, Halifax sat far from the west coast where Chinese numbers were high and anti-Chinese racism at its fiercest. Yet racial violence erupted on the east coast too. Although, from past to present, Halifax's Chinese experience has very much reflected the local setting, it has also closely resembled that of other Chinese-Canadian communities.

*The Ling children at their North End farm, c1935.*

**Wah Sing Does Washing**

In November 1890, two Chinese arrived in Halifax to explore possibilities in the laundry business. They opened a shop on Duke Street and summoned their compatriots. All were members of Wah Kee, a laundry firm with branches in Montreal and other cities. One member travelled on to Truro to start another branch.[1] Business in Halifax must have proved profitable because another laundry opened on Duke Street in 1894. Its owner was related to Wah Kee's proprietor and also hailed from Montreal. The new shop was called

**SAM WAH LAUNDRY.**

5 Bliss St., Halifax, N. S.

Telephone B 6940.

When wanted ..................................... Street

$

WE CALL FOR AND DELIVER.

| Gentlemen's | Ladies' |
|---|---|
| Shirts.................15. | Shirt waists, plain 15 to 25. |
| Shirts, silk, flannel 20 to 25. | Shirt waists, fancy 25 to 35. |
| Shirts, dress..........25. | Dresses...........35 to 1.00. |
| Collars...............3. | Skirts.............20 to 60. |
| Cuffs, pair............6. | Petticoats........10 to 30. |
| Night Shirts......10 to 15. | Chemises.........10 to 20. |
| Drawers...........8 to 10. | Slip Waists........5 to 15. |
| Undershirts.......8 to 10. | Night Gowns......10 to 20. |
| Combinations....18 to 20. | Aprons...........12 to 20. |
| Socks, pair...........5. | Drawers..........8 to 15. |
| Handkerchiefs........2½. | Belts...............5. |
| Handkerchiefs, silk....4. | Bibs...............5. |
| Ties...............5 to 10. | Collars with Capes 5 to 10. |
| Coats............20 to 35. | Combinations....12 to 15. |
| Vests............20 to 25. | Undershirts..........3. |
| Pants............35 to 50. | Stockings, per pair....6. |
| Fronts...............8. | Handkerchiefs.......2. |
| Pajama Suits.........20. | Coats............25 to 50. |
| Aprons..............10. | |
| Towels.............4 to 6. | **Miscellaneous** |
| Sweaters............25. | |
| Overalls.........50 to 75. | Table Cloths....15 to 35. |
| B. V. D........10 to 15. | Toilet Covers....5 to 20. |
| Muffler.............10. | Napkins..............3. |
| Robes..............25. | Sheets..........10 to 15. |
| | Pillow Slips.........5. |
| **Children's** | Pillow Shams, Pair....20. |
| | Rollers...........7 to 10. |
| Dresses..........16 to 35. | Bed Spreads.....20 to 35. |
| Skirts...........10 to 20. | Quilts............40 to 75. |
| Waists............5 to 20. | Blankets, flannel 20 to 40. |
| Drawers..........5 to 15. | Blankets, wool..40 to 75. |
| Night Dresses...10 to 15. | Curtains, pair...35 to 75. |
| Pants..........10 to 15. | Towels............4 to 10. |
| Baby Bonnets........10. | |

**Master Workmanship. Prompt Service. Reasonable Prices.**

**Notify us immediately on all errors. Your cooperation will be greatly appreciated.**

**We will not be responsible for any damage to worn out or discoloring materials.**

**Special quick service can be given if necessary.**

Washing Days:—Monday, Wednesday and Friday mornings.

Kindly recommend us to your friends.

*Price list for laundry services, 1910.*

Wah Sing, and the local newspaper noted cheerfully that it "might almost be pronounced wash-ing."[2] Fong Choy was another enterprising Chinese from Montreal who came to start a laundry in 1895. But he went on to St. John's to start yet another washhouse before heading to Bermuda.

The Chinese population in Nova Scotia rose from 106 in 1901 to 134 in 1911. But growth was not steady because tallies rose and fell according to the ups and downs of the economy.[3] Meanwhile Halifax's Chinese interacted with whites through the churches and police, but in different ways.

The first groups among Halifax's Chinese were church-oriented. St. Paul's Anglican Church offered English classes as early as 1903. By 1905 the Chinese Sunday school and night classes had 25 students and many volunteer teachers.[4] More churches joined in and also supported famine relief in China in 1912.[5] Grateful for such generosity, 50 Chinese students held a banquet for their Christian friends in 1914 at Carleton House, featuring music, readings and toasts.[6]

Encounters with the police involved gambling. In 1906, when a clergyman claimed poorer Chinese were losing large sums ($300 to $700) at the gambling tables, authorities charged one Chinese with running a game-house.[7] Forty-two Chinese were arrested in 1909; three were fined for gambling

and 22 for just watching. The punishment was $20 each, or two months in prison.[8]

**No Free Lunch**

Anti-Chinese hostility increased with the economic downturn at the end of the Great War. Moreover, the Chinese presence downtown had grown: two Chinese grocery stores and halls for the Lee Family Association, the KMT (Nationalists) and Chinese Freemasons in the Granville/Salter area; and Chinese-run cafés and laundries on Grafton, Hollis and Sackville streets. Quong Oon Tai and Wing Shang Lung sold Chinese and Japanese goods on Gottingen and Barrington streets.[9]

Another factor was Halifax harbour, the world's second-deepest port, ice-free all year round. It supported port and military facilities that required sailors and soldiers. Unfortunately, unruly soldiers posed a problem to the Chinese.

In May 1918 soldiers hauled a Chinese laundryman from his shop and beat him when he insisted on a check stub before returning their laundry. The police arrived but arrested nobody.[10] Early next year, drunken soldiers refused to pay the bill after eating an expensive meal at a Sackville Street café. When the Chinese proprietor went to call the police, the soldiers pushed over the tables and a fight ensued.[11]

In 1919 a major riot erupted against Chinese cafés. Several hundred soldiers and civilians rampaged for two hours through six downtown cafés, sweeping down Gottingen Street and onto Barrington. The mob smashed chairs, tables and plate glass windows; they trashed and looted cash registers, and shattered cigar cases to steal the contents. The Frisco Café only escaped damage because the proprietor's white wife stood at the door and defied the rioters. People leaving nearby theatres crowded after the mob for a taste of the action. The enormous crowd left local police unable to help until military police arrived.[12]

The cafés suffered $15,000 in damages,[13] but city council accepted no liability. The Chinese consul was referred to the federal government instead, and the struggle for compensation lasted for years.[14] Several Chinese lost everything but the clothes they were wearing. Some whites blamed the Chinese for bringing the riot upon themselves because a typical shopkeeper was seen to be making money here, but spending little here and sending most of his funds back to China.[15]

The English teachers of the Chinese responded:

*One absurd reason which was given was that "some of the Chinamen were growing rich." This is certainly no excuse, and even if true, any money possessed by the men attacked had been gained by hard work and thrift, not by taking advantage of public necessity to charge exorbitant prices, nor by selling that which ruins men, body and soul. On the contrary they give full value for money received. Can this be truly said of all Halifax men who have "grown rich?"[16]*

The dust had barely settled when another battle erupted. A man started arguing with the Busy Bee Café's owner and then wrecked furniture, broke dishes and hurled the cash register through the window. Again, a crowd of bystanders began to push in, some shouting "hit her up." But police gained control, and damage was limited to $300.[17]

A grand jury was appointed to investigate. Its report called for cooperation between civil and military police to stop any future "uprisings."[18] Nevertheless, from December 1919 to August 1920, there were at least four more attacks when whites fought Chinese staff or damaged café property after refusing to pay for meals.[19] Soldiers or veterans were involved in half these incidents. Some whites believed foreigners controlled the restaurant trade, but the city found that the Chinese actually ran only 19 of the city's 55 restaurants, where they employed 145 of their people.[20]

*Ngoon Lee, who emigrated to Halifax in 1906, with his son, Shew Chuck Lee at the age of nine, and Lee Wye Ark, Chuck's guardian, in a 1916 studio portrait.*

Chinese laundrymen were also harassed. The Halifax Herald featured a 1919 article, "Why Should Chinamen Do Canadian Laundry?" which urged whites to regain control of the laundry trade. It recounted how the situation had evolved:

*Laundry went out of the homes to be done elsewhere, because it was heavy work that could be detached without any detriment to the general plan of work and with a great saving of the strength of the housewife or housekeeper. Until recent years this work was done by Canadian women in homes and in the city laundry. Then came the Chinamen and much of the labor went to them. The work took on the color of the laborer and the Canadian seemed to feel that there was something degrading in it.*[21]

In the next decade, Chinese cafés were still targeted by the law. In 1923, two restaurant owners and six white women were charged with prostitution, but the case against the Chinese was dismissed.[22] The following year, the restaurant owners petitioned the legislature against a bill that called for tearing down booths and stalls in dining halls.[23] (The legislation did not pass.) In the last half of 1929, police carried out several raids in Chinese premises, charging the Chinese with possession of opium.[24]

### Community Life

*A water pipe for smoking tobacco.*

After three Chinese were killed in the disastrous munitions explosion that claimed 1963 lives in 1917, the larger Chinatowns reminded Halifax's Chinese that their small community was not alone. The Vancouver Chinese Benevolent Association sent $100 in aid. Montreal, of course, was a closer connection. Maritime Chinese travelled there to its Chinese Hospital for treatment. And the busy railway routes made it possible for Montreal to supply foodstuffs to the Atlantic Chinese, both to companies and to individual families.[25]

Families were few among Halifax's Chinese. Not until June 1920 was the city's first Chinese baby born, to a Lee family

running a laundry on Bliss Street.[26] The following year, only two Chinese women were recorded in the city's census, giving Halifax's Chinese the highest male-to-female ratio in Canada, at sixty-to-one. But not all Chinese men were "bachelors" because some lived with Acadian women.

These women had trekked in from rural Nova Scotia looking for jobs. They found work as waitresses in Chinese-run cafés, and then befriended the staff. They may have been just as lonely as the migrants from Asia, and the couples gave birth to mixed-race children.[27] This was likely one reason why Chinese restaurant owners organized fundraising in 1929 in expectation of provincial laws forbidding Chinese employers to hire white women.[28] The male-to-female situation had improved by 1941: the twenty Chinese women then in the community changed the ratio to five to one.

Halifax's Chinese embraced a variety of causes. A Chinese YMCA was formed in 1920 and held monthly meetings.[29] The Chinese Freemasons honoured their Five Founders in annual celebrations. On the first anniversary of the exclusion law in 1924, Halifax's Chinese observed Humiliation Day in concert with fellow countrymen across Canada. Robert Wong, the English-language secretary of the local KMT, said, "We do not ask any special favors over immigrants of other nationalities entering Canada from the immigration authorities, but we do want fair-play."[30] That same year, Chinese from Vancouver solicited funds for a high school in Hoi-ping, the home district of many Halifax Chinese. In 1925, after the anti-foreign May 30 Shanghai Incident, Halifax Chinese raised $1200 for victims wounded by British-led police.[31]

In 1931, 77 percent of Halifax's Chinese community was Christian, the highest proportion of any Canadian city. Ten years later, that percentage remained high, at 66 percent.[32] But Chinese-language congregations did not form as they did elsewhere.

When war between China and Japan was declared in 1937, Halifax Chinese donated funds through a local branch of the National Salvation Association. The city's Chinese called for everyone to donate at least $10 in three months' time for an airplane fund.[33] A month later, they sent a telegram to General Chiang Kai-shek, urging him to fight the Japanese until victory.[34] In later years, they sold Chinese war bonds, raised funds for refugee relief, and marked important dates such as July 7, the day a Chinese general finally resisted Japanese advances instead of retreating.

**Family Stories**

Chinese families provided a thread of continuity in a community unsettled by the periodic return of its men to China. Heads of Chinese families often tried different jobs before settling down. For example, How Ling left Winnipeg in 1918 and arrived in New Glasgow, Nova Scotia, where his family grew wheat and oats, tended cattle, and ran a laundry as well. They later farmed in Brookside before moving on to Halifax, where they set up a farm to raise Chinese vegetables and chickens at the north end of Gottingen Street, overlooking Africville. But in 1941, the family changed occupations and opened the Imperial Café on Upper Water Street.[35]

One Lee family brought Halifax's early Chinese history into the present. Ngoon Lee came to Halifax in 1906, assisted by relatives surnamed Fong who were already here. A few years later, he went to China to visit his family and a son Shew Chuck (Chuck) was born. Back in Halifax, Ngoon Lee opened his own laundry on Bliss Street in 1910. He returned to China again in 1916 and came back with his nine-year-old son. Chuck Lee grew up as the only Chinese boy in town.

Chuck spoke about his first experiences in Canada:

*I did not start school right away because of my limited English. There was a Theakston family on 56 Seymour Street that took a great interest in me. They took me into their home as one of their own. I also played with the boys in the immediate neighbourhood. Pretty soon I acquired a working knowledge in English and by September I enrolled at LeMarchant Street School. Initially I was treated with mixed feelings. Some treated me with curiosity, others with hatred, and a small percentage went out of the way to make me feel comfortable.[36]*

After ten years, Chuck went home to get married, and became inspired to help in that country's modernization:

*When I was in China, I witnessed many changes within the ten years that I was away. Many physical changes were evident such as new roads, communications by telephone and telegraph, electric generating plants and so on. In Canton city slums were cleared and shopping districts were modernized. China appeared to be vibrant and full of new hope. ... I, too, was very enthusiastic at the time. I wanted to contribute my share towards the modernization of China. I thought I could do something in the construction end. With this in mind, I selected engineering as my profession.'[37]*

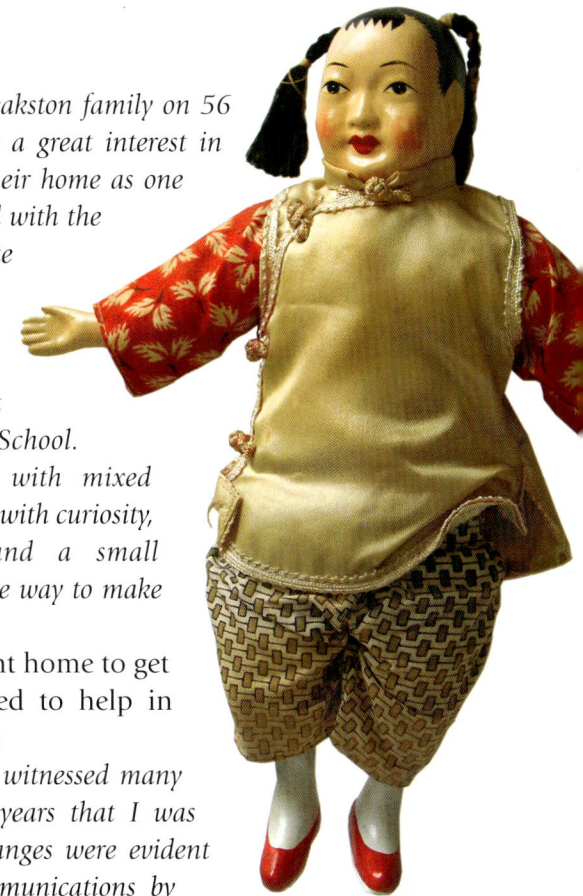

*A Chinese doll*

After graduating from the Nova Scotia Technical College (later Dalhousie Technology) as a civil engineer (the first of his

*How Ling's family opened a café on Upper Water Street in 1941.*

race to do so from any Nova Scotia university) the situation was very different:

> *Of course my original intention was to go back to China after graduation, but we were at war with Japan since 1937. The sea lanes around China were blockaded and I could not go back. The white society here would not welcome me in the professional field, so virtually I was a man without a country. … When they did not even take your address and telephone number it was obvious they were not interested. To use an old cliché, I had only "a Chinaman's chance." I had to swallow my pride and worked in a restaurant to survive.*[38]

During the war, the government's Wartime Housing Project hired him as an engineer, and after that he worked for the CNR, the airport and the aircraft refurbishing company, Clark Ruse.[39]

## Restaurants Boom

The post-war years heralded many changes, as in Chinese communities across Canada. Chinese-run restaurants had flourished during the war thanks to Halifax's many military functions, and by 1952 they numbered 44. The city's population had grown as factory work expanded for the war effort. In 1944 Quon Fong opened the Garden View Restaurant, a dining hall that boasted the largest menu of Chinese and Canadian cuisine east of Montreal.[40]

With the citizenship changes in 1947, the wives and children of longtime residents could finally come to Canada. Chuck Lee sponsored his wife and daughter in 1948 after long years of separation. In other families, sons came to join their fathers, and then returned to China to find brides. Donald Lee came in 1948 to work in his father's laundry and then brought a bride back in 1953. A Chinese-language school opened for Canadian-born children. The Chinese community began to grow, rising from 372 in 1941 to 637 in 1961.

But one mainstay of Halifax's Chinese foundered. In 1967, Donald Lee closed his father's laundry when he found that customers preferred to use coin-operated laundromats, even though his company did good work and customers were pleased. Lee knew that it would not be easy to find another job, but knew he had to in order to give his children a good education.[41]

Restaurants boomed as Chinese cuisine became more popular, and they provided opportunities for new immigrants. Freeman Hum came in 1950 and worked as a waiter for years before opening a restaurant with 21 staff. Later, he opened Halifax's first Chinese drive-in and take-out service, as well as restaurants in Dartmouth and Spryfield.

*Halifax's Chinese community on Grafton Street, VJ Day, 1945.*

**New Immigration**

After 1967, when independent Chinese immigration resumed, the influx changed Halifax's Chinese. No longer a homogeneous community descended from South China peasants, it embraced diverse newcomers with different languages and higher levels of education. In 1969, newcomers formed the Halifax Chinese Christian Church, a non-denominational church, at Central Baptist Church. At first it attracted doctors who were practising in Halifax for their Canadian licences. Then students from Hong Kong boosted the congregation, and prompted the church to take an active role in supporting newly arrived foreign students.

Halifax, home to seven degree-granting universities and colleges plus several research institutes, attracted scholars from

*Albert Lee imitating how other children taunted him, 1960s.*

Taiwan, China and other parts of Asia. They in turn formed Chinese student and faculty groups, or applied for landed status and Canadian citizenship. They introduced more Chinese culture to Halifax. For example, at Chinese New Year in 1970, the Chinese Students Association presented Halifax's first Chinese lion dance. By 1981 Halifax's Chinese population was about 1000. A few years later, Celebration, an annual multicultural festival was initiated. Local groups such as the Chinese Society of Nova Scotia and the Chinese Benevolent Society worked together at these events.

Immigration from Mainland China increased in the mid-1990s, and the Halifax Chinese Christian Church soon found that a third of its members were from there. The church helped foreign students by directing them to public services, Chinese grocers, and free lodging and computer access.[42] By 2000, it was estimated that half of Halifax's 4000 Chinese were foreign students.[43]

New influxes of Chinese were seen in different ways. Small family-run cafés gave way to well-financed restaurants with larger and grander dining halls. More of the city's medical and science professionals were Chinese.[44] The Halifax Chinese Language School (for Mandarin) started in 1993. Asian shops and restaurants appeared on Quinpool Road, and local businesspeople hoped in vain it might become a more dynamic Chinatown.[45] In 1998 Halifax held its first annual dragon boat races, sponsored by Aliant Telecom at Lake Banook in Dartmouth. The 2002 races raised $130,000 for the Nova Scotia Amateur Sport Fund.

For Chinese immigrants in Halifax, as for many other Maritime residents, jobs were hard to find. Settlement workers noted that some employment services were not available locally.[46] When local graduates moved away, their parents joined them upon retirement, further limiting Chinese population growth.[47] Other immigrants looked for jobs in

Vancouver or Toronto, where they could be part of larger Chinese communities.

In 1997 photojournalist Albert Lee (Ngoon Lee's grandson and Chuck Lee's son) organized the exhibition Growing Up Chinese in Halifax at the Museum of Natural History. For the show he borrowed photographs and memorabilia from the core Chinese families. It received glowing reviews.

In 2001 Chinese Canadians were only 10 percent of Halifax's visible minorities, while African-Canadians were 52 percent and Arab Canadians 12 percent. Chuck Lee noted: "Chinese Canadians have benefited by the black people's struggle against racism. The blacks acted as vanguards in the fight against bigotry and oppression. We Chinese were not so vocal, we mainly jumped on their band-wagon. We should be thankful to the blacks for their success and join them in the common struggle for equality and freedom."[48]

*Chuck Lee grew up as the only Chinese boy in town, 1988.*

# CONCLUSION

In the past, cities witnessed ugly acts of anti-Chinese hostility as well as intense participation in political issues and cultural activities. Recently, new life has been breathed into many older Chinatowns, and new Chinatowns have brought new life to Canadian cities.

Today, the process of immigration continues to be played out in cities, as newcomers re-settle and strive to integrate into the mainstream. In recent years, Chinese immigrants have been the most numerous of new arrivals to Canada. This raises their visibility when issues around resettlement, official languages, Chinese-themed businesses and race relations make the news. Such issues are to be expected in an environment of rapid change, where governments and ethnic groups expect newcomers to adapt quickly and make contributions.

The internal diversity of Chinese communities is their most striking feature. There is much variety in homelands, arrival dates, official language ability, degree of integration, community participation, and other variables. But these differences are less visible than the by now familiar elements of the urban landscape such as Chinatowns, Asian-themed malls, Chinese restaurants, Chinese Cultural Centres and dragon boat races, all of which are seen as natural parts of Canada's multicultural diversity.

The fortunes of the Chinese in Canada were always closely tied to the well-being of their new land. The laundries and restaurants of the past depended on local customers; contemporary immigrants seek wider opportunities in business, science, education and the arts. Even the two general types of Chinatowns reflect trends in Canadian urban growth. One model is descended from original Chinatowns located downtown, which used to be the focal point of cities. The other model, suburban, involves Asian-themed commercial centres that offer goods and services to an increasingly multicultural population.

Although Chinese settlement in Canada also involved small towns across the country, it was in the cities that community development took place. Given that increasing numbers of Canadians live in cities today, it is there that the greatest integration of Chinese and non-Chinese occurs. In the future, urban centres will continue to be the engines of growth, and Chinese Canadians will seek to contribute to them their unique skills and cultures.

It is there that the next chapter of Chinese-Canadian history will be written.

# ENDNOTES

## INTRODUCTION

1  Marlon Hom, Songs of Gold Mountain (Berkeley: University of California Press, 1987) 126.
2  Canada. Royal Commission on Chinese and Japanese Immigration, Sessional Paper 54, 1902, 235, 237.
3  Ibid., 236.
4  Ibid., 278.

## VICTORIA

1  David Chuenyan Lai, Chinatowns: Towns within Cities in Canada (Vancouver: UBC Press, 1988), 187.
2  Edgar Wickberg, ed., From China to Canada (Toronto: McClelland & Stewart, 1982), 13–14.
3  James Morton, In the Sea of Sterile Mountains (Vancouver: J.J. Douglas, 1973), 10.
4  The Colonist, 5 April 1864.
5  Charles P. Sedgwick, "The Context of Economic Change and Continuity in an Urban Overseas Chinese Community," MA thesis, University of Victoria, 1973, 72–73.
6  Lai, Chinatowns, 196.
7  Lai, Chinatowns, 189.
8  David Chuenyan Lai, "The Chinese Consolidated Benevolent Association in Victoria: Its Origins and Functions," B.C. Studies 15(1975), 55.
9  Lai, "Benevolent Association," 57–58.
10 David Chuenyan Lai, "Chinese Attempts to Discourage Emigration to Canada: Some Findings from the Chinese Archives in Victoria," B.C. Studies 18 (Summer 1973), 35, 37.
11 This account is from David Chuenyan Lai, "The Issue of Discrimination in Education in Victoria, 1901–1923," Canadian Ethnic Studies 19 (1987), 47–67.
12 Colonist, 6 April 1904.

13 Colonist, 16 Nov. 1899.
14 Lai, Chinatowns, 242.
15 Sedgwick, "Economic Change," 139, 172–173.
16 David Chuenyan Lai, "A 'Prison' for Chinese Immigrants," The Asianadian 2 No. 4: 18–19.
17 Victoria Daily Times, 12 Aug. 1939.
18 Marjorie Wong, The Dragon and the Maple Leaf (London, Ontario: Pirie Press, 1994), 36–38.
19 Lai, Chinatowns, 240.
20 Lai, Chinatowns, 240–243.
21 Martin Segger, "Requiem for Chinatown," Victoria's Monday Magazine, 28 March–3 April 1977.
22 Derek Sidemius, "Victoria Chinatown: Cultural Mecca for Immigrants," Victoria Times Colonist (hereafter VTC), reprinted in Chinatown News (hereafter CN) 18 July 1983.
23 Richard Watts, "Chinatown casino pitch causes split," VTC, 12 Dec. 1997:1
24 "Boat people get little sympathy in Chinese community," VTC, 13 Aug. 1999:A3.
25 Cindy Harnett, "Treatment of migrants riles some," VTC, 23 July 1977:D1.
26 Craig McInnes, "Immigration tidal wave bypassed the island," Globe and Mail (hereafter GM), 21 April 1997:A2.

## VANCOUVER

1  Canada. Royal Commission on Chinese and Japanese Immigration, Sessional Papers 54, 1902, 155.
2  Royal Commission, 1902, 176.
3  Daphne Marlatt and Carole Itter, eds., "Opening Doors: Vancouver's East End," Sound Heritage 8 (1979):40.
4  Jung Hong-Len was interviewed by Theresa Low for the Provincial Archives of British Columbia, June–July 1980.
5  Dick Yip, interview, 1987.
6  Foon Sien, "Letter to Santa," CN, 18 Dec. 1954.
7  CN, 3 Aug. 1962:3.
8  John Kirkwood, "Vancouver's Chinatown in

Ferment," Vancouver Province, reprinted in CN, 3 Apr. 1971:14.
9  See Frances Bula, "Asian money in B.C.: racism and real estate: getting the real story," in Bulletin, Centre for Investigative Journalism (Spring 1989):9.
10 Gillian Shaw, "Investment anger confuses Hong Kong," Vancouver Sun, 18 March 1989:A1.
11 Dave McCullough, "The Review stands by its readers," Richmond Review, 28 Feb. 1996.
12 Rod Mickleburgh, "After 6, it's like a ghost town," GM, 17 Feb. 1999:A1.
13 Hugh Xiaobing Tan, "Controversy over Dim Sum Diaries," Canada and Hong Kong Update (Fall, 1991):5.

## CALGARY

1  "The Chinatown as seen by a reporter," Calgary Herald (hereafter CH) 22 Sept. 1909.
2  "The segregation of the Chinese," CH, 5 Oct. 1910.
3  Luey Kheang, "Why are they suitable for heaven?" CH, 7 Oct. 1910.
4  "Official opinion of Chinese puzzle," CH, 13 Oct. 1910.
5  J. Brian Dawson, "Mooncakes in Gold Mountain" (Calgary: Detselig, 1991), 55, 65.
6  Oi Kwan Foundation, Commemorative Book (Calgary, 1987), 39.
7  Mr. Buck Doo Yee was interviewed by June Yee and Richard Wong, July 1974. Glenbow Archives, Chinese Canadian Heritage Program, Tape 1A, p.1.
8  Dushan Bresky, "Personality of the week,"CH, 18 Dec. 1954.
9  Grady Semmens, "Stamps legend tackled feelings of being different," CH 6 May 2001
10 Dawson, Mooncakes, 212
11 Marjorie Wong, Dragon and Maple Leaf, 90.
12 Helen Chan, "Family organization and change among the Chinese in Calgary," MA thesis, University of Calgary, 1980:23.
13 Paul Juhl, "Calgary plans new Chinatown," Calgary Albertan, reprinted in CN, 18 March 1966:38.

14 Sien Lok Society of Calgary. National Conference on Urban Renewal and its Effects on Chinatown, Calgary, 1969:31.

15 Jill Stewart, "Hong Kong exodus boosts Calgary jobs," CH, 29 Dec. 1996:A1

16 Ibid.

17 Stephen Ewart, "Chinese roughnecks learn ways of Alberta oilpatch," CH, 13 June 1998.

18 Wendy-Anne Thompson, "Helping build Cultural Bridges," CH, 12 Dec. 1999: D1

19 Jacqueline Louie, "Chinese Cultural Centre hub of constant activity," CH, 13 Sept. 1999.

20 Joe Woodard, "But she was a feminist racist: a columnist has some startling words about the Famous Five," Alberta Report, 18 May 1998:38.

21 Jacqueline Louie, "Chinese Cultural Centre hub of constant activity," CH, 13 Sept. 1999.

22 Joe Woodard, "But she was a feminist racist: a columnist has some startling words about the Famous Five," Alberta Report, 18 May 1998:38.

## WINNIPEG

1 Gaylene Dempsey, "Get Down to Chinatown," Winnipeg Life, Spring 2004

2 Wickberg, China to Canada, 92.

3 Lai, Chinatowns, 95.

4 Winnipeg Free Press (hereafter WFP), 20 May 1922:5.

5 Wing-sam Chow, "A Chinese Community in a Prairie City: A Holistic Perspective of its Class and Ethnic Relations," Ph.D. dissertation, Michigan State University, 1981, 68–69.

6 Ibid., 67.

7 WFP, 26 April 1911: 28.

8 Chinese Times (hereafter CT), 7, 8 & 9 April 1917, held at University of British Columbia, Main Library, Special Collections, Chinese Canadian Research Collection (hereafter CCRC) box 4 file 6; CT, 26 Feb. 1919 in CCRC box 4 file 8; CT, 21 Jan. 1922 in CCRC box 4 file 11.

9 C. Millien, E. Woo, P. Yeh, Winnipeg Chinese (Ottawa, Department of the Secretary of State, 1971)

10 Chow, "Chinese Community," 68.

11 Ivy Huffman and Julia Kwong, The Dream of Gold Mountain (Winnipeg: Hyperion, 1991), 71–72.

12 WFP, 10 Nov. 1915:5.

13 WFP, 23 Aug. 1915:5.

14 CT 23 Oct. 1915, in CCRC 4:4.

15 CT 28 Jan., 4 Feb. 1916, in CCRC 4:5.

16 CT, 6 Nov. 1917.

17 CT, 13, 18 June 1923, in CCRC 2:1,4:13.

18 CT, 5 May 1924 in CCRC 4:14.

19 Huffman and Kwong, Dream of Gold Mountain, 11.

20 Winnipeg Tribune (hereafter WT), 4 Nov, 1931:1, 18.

21 Ibid.

22 WFP, 14 Sept. 1931; WT, 4 Nov. 1931.

23 Chow, "Chinese Community," 67–69.

24 Ellen Chan, "Planning for Change: The Winnipeg Chinese Community and its Responsiveness to Government Services," Master of City Planning thesis, University of Manitoba, 1978:90.

25 Julia Kwong, "Transformation of an ethnic community: from a national to a cultural community" in Ujimoto, K. Victor and G. Hirabayashi, Asian Canadians & Multiculturalism: Selections from the proceedings, Asian Canadian Symposium IV, Université de Montréal, Montreal, Quebec, 1980:92.

26 Chow, "Chinese Community," 68–69.

27 WFP, 16 Dec. 1937:1, 2.

28 WFP, 20 March 1939.

29 CT, 18 June 1941.

30 Wickberg, China to Canada, 193.

31 WFP, 30 July 1947:3.

32 Bob Metcalfe, "Chinese newcomer tells of extortion," WT, 3 Dec. 1951.

33 CN, 3 Sept. 1959:10.

34 WT, 26 March 1946.

35 Chan, "Planning for Change," 82.

36 CN, 3 Oct. 1968:18, 19.

37 Brian Pardoe, "Chinatown will be Chinatown," WT, 25 Jan. 1980.

38 WFP, 21 Feb. 1977.

39 Chan, "Planning for Change," 84.

40 Ibid., 114–118.

41 Chow, "Chinese Community," 89.

42 Myron Love, "Winnipeg's $14M New Chinatown Development Nearing Completion," CN 18 Jan. 1987:14.

43 Dave Haynes, "Chinatown struggles for identity," WFP, 14 July 1982.

44 CN, 3 Sept. 1985:28.

45 Greg Bannister, "Manitoba finds largest outside source of new capital," WFP 1 March 1987:20.

46 Michael Bociurkiw, "Hong Kong investors change plans," WFP, 22 July 1988: 51.

## TORONTO

1 Peter Kwong, Chinatown, N.Y.: Labor & Politics, 1930–1950, (New York: Monthly Review Press, 1979), 24.

2 Dora Nipp, "The Chinese in Toronto: in Robert Harney, ed., Gathering Places: Peoples and Neighbourhoods of Toronto 1834–1945, (Toronto, Multicultural History Society of Ontario, 1985), 149.

3 Jeff Watson, "The Chinese in Early Toronto: 1877–1930," Polyphony 15:13.

4 Nipp, "Chinese in Toronto," 156, 163.

5 K. Paupst, "A Note on Anti-Chinese Sentiment in Toronto before the First World War," Canadian Ethnic Studies 9 (1977):56.

6 CT, 23, 25 Jan. 1915 in CCRC 4:1.

7 CT, 11 Feb. 1918 in CCRC 4:7; CT, 20 Feb. 1919, in CCRC 4:8; 16 Nov. 1920, in CCRC 4:9.

8 Jack Canuck, 28 Oct. 1911:11.

9 Jack Canuck, 16 Sept. 1911:10.

10 Nipp, "Chinese in Toronto," 154.

11 Ibid., 154–155.

12 Wickberg, China to Canada, 107.

13 Ibid., 143.

14 CT, 2 June 1916 in CCRC 4:5.

15 CT, 21 Jan. 1930 in CCRC 4:19.

16 Nipp, "Chinese in Toronto," 170.

17 Wickberg, China to Canada, 192.

18 Watson, "Chinese in Early Toronto," 15.

19 Saturday Night Magazine, 25 May 1907:2.

20 Watson, "Chinese in Early Toronto," 16.
21 Valerie Mah, "Early Chinatown," Polyphony 6 (1984):35.
22 Cheng Ying-wai, in Richard H. Thompson, Toronto's Chinatown: The Changing Social Organization of an Ethnic Community (New York: AMS Press, Inc., 1989) 105–106.
23 Margaret Daly, 'Save Toronto's Chinatown fight on,' Toronto Star (hereafter TS), reprinted in Chinatown News, 3 April 1969:12.
24 Dick Beddoes, "Soy hits fan in Chinatown," GM, 6 April 1977.
25 R.H. Thompson, Toronto's Chinatown, 358.
26 Shugang Wang, New Development Patterns of Chinese Commercial Activity in the Toronto CMA, (Toronto: Ryerson Polytechnic University, 1996), 7.
27 TS, 8, 14, 22, 29 Jan. 1994.
28 Royson James, "New Chinatown springs up in Scarborough," TS, reprinted in CN, 3 March 1987:4.
29 CN, 3 Aug.1986:28.
30 TS, 29 April 1991: A7; 2 May 1991:ES02.
31 Maureen Murray, "Markham: can good salesmanship turn into racism?" TS, 27 Aug. 1995:F1.
32 Ibid.
33 Peter Krivel, "Racism blocks Chinese malls, developer says," TS, 22 Sept. 1995:NY1.
34 Peter Krivel, "Chinese heritage group won't talk to ratepayers after racism claims," TS, 8 Dec. 1995:NY 5.
35 Valerie Preston and Lucia Lo, "Asian theme' malls in suburban Toronto: land use conflict in Richmond Hill," Canadian Geographer 44 (2000):182–90.
36 Business Journal, October 1991:22.
37 Winnie Ng, "The organization of Chinese restaurant workers," Polyphony 15:41–45.
38 Wear Fair Action Kit, Issue Sheet #1, Sept. 1977.
39 Jen Ross, "Garment work turns homes into sweatshops," GM, 21 June 1999:A7.
40 Guang Tian, Chinese-Canadians, Canadian Chinese: Coping and Adapting in North America (Lewiston: Edwin Mellen Press, 1999), 229.

## OTTAWA

1 Li, Qiang, "Ethnic Minority Churches: the Case of the Chinese Christian Churches in Ottawa," Ph.D. dissertation, University of Ottawa, 2000:123.
2 CT, 14 Jan.1915 in CCRC 4/1.
3 Jean-Guy Daigle, "From Survival to Success: the Chinese in 20th Century Ottawa," unpublished paper, 2000:9.
4 CT, 28 May 1917 in CCRC 4/6.
5 CT, 2 May 1916 in CCRC 4/5.
6 Wickberg, China to Canada, 107.
7 CT, 27 Mar 1919 in CCRC 4/8.
8 CT, 28 Dec 1920 in CCRC 4/9.
9 Interviews at Chinese Freemasons' Ottawa Branch, 1973, in CCRC 10/61.
10 CT, 20 Feb. 1915 in CCRC 4/1.
11 CT, 27 Feb. 1919 in CCRC 4/8.
12 CT, 17 Nov 1920 in CCRC 2/1.
13 CT, 8 Feb. 1921 in CCRC 2/1.
14 Daigle, "Survival to Success," 6.
15 Ottawa Citizen (hereafter OC), 9 Dec. 1996.
16 Daigle, "Survival to Success," 13.
17 Fisher, Stephen, "Changing Patterns of Social Organization among the Chinese in Ottawa: A Study of Internal and External Determinants," Ph.D dissertation, Carleton University, 1979:145.
18 Li, "Ethnic Minority Churches," 141.
19 Ibid., 140.
20 Daigle, "Survival to Success," 20.
21 Li, "Ethnic Minority Churches," 142.
22 CN, 3 Sept. 1968: 30.
23 Fisher, "Changing Patterns," 284.
24 Ibid.
25 Jacquie Miller, "The Chinese: a diverse group with common threads," OC 5 July 1986:F1.
26 Daigle, "Survival to Success," 27.
27 Li, "Ethnic Minority Church," 181–187
28 Kathryn May, "Pacific Rim investment in Canada; Ottawa," OC, 17 Jan. 1989:B1.
29 James Bagnell, "Going home: Booming China makes a play for ex-pats burned by North America's tech recession," OC, 6 Mar 2003:F4.
30 Karen Laurison, "Bloodbath in Beijing; Ottawa protesters lay wreaths for dead," OC, 5 June 1989:A5.
31 Sandee Wong, "Hundreds protest NATO bombings," OC, 12 May 1999:F1.

## MONTREAL

1 Kwok Bun Chan, "Smoke and Fire: The Chinese in Quebec, Canada c1863-1987," typescript, c1987, 29.
2 Montreal Star, 1 July 1888.
3 Denise Helly, Les Chinois à Montréal, 1877–1951, (Quebec: Institut Québécois de recherche sur la culture, 1987), 82, 84.
4 Ibid., 65–67.
5 Ibid., 65, 67–69.
6 Helly, 67–68.
7 Chinese Neighbourhood Society of Montreal, "A History of Chinese Community in Montreal," c1990, 14.
8 CT, 6, 9,15 Feb., 31 May, 21 July 1915 in CCRC 4/3.
9 Helly, Chinois à Montréal, 121.
10 Ibid., 230
11 Chan, "Smoke and Fire," 239–240.
12 Edith Eaton, "Girl slave in Montreal," Montreal Daily Witness, 4 May 1894.
13 Wickberg, China to Canada, 114.
14 Montreal Gazette (hereafter MG), 15 Dec. 1933.
15 Mary Janigan, "Inside Montreal's Chinatown," reprinted from MG in CN, 18 May 1973.
16 Helly, Chinois à Montréal, 172–173
17 Evi Kwong-ming Ko, "The Montreal Chinese Hospital 1919-1982," McGill University, MA Thesis, 1984, 50.
18 Helly, Chinois à Montréal, 257–258.
19 "Arthur Lee: Noodles are his Bag," CN 18 Jan. 1969: 9, 13
20 "Montreal's Dynamic Chinese Food Industry," from En Ville Weekly, reprinted in CN 3 Sept. 1970:17.
21 Nicolas Van Praet, "Wong Wing sells out to McCain's," MG, 4 Oct. 2002: B1.
22 Jacques Hamilton, "Chinatowns facing extinc-

tion," reprinted in CN, 3 April 1970:4–7.

23 Bernice Kwong, "Montreal Que.," CN, 3 May 1972:58.

24 Michael Doyle, "Development Dooms Montreal Churches," CN, 3 Oct. 1972:14.

25 Chan, "Smoke and Fire," 362–365.

26 Jack Todd, "Montreal's Chinatown still fighting City Hall," MG, reprinted CN, 18 Nov. 1987:5.

27 Ibid.

28 Sheila McGovern, "A very lonely generation," MG, 30 Jan. 2003:A1.

29 "Chinese Canadians in the News," CN, 3 July 1969:39.

30 Montreal Star, 19 Feb. 1977:A6.

31 South China Morning Post, 3 July 1977.

32 MG, 21 Feb. 1984:A1.

33 Shirley Won, "Quebec hustling to win business from Hong Kong," MG, 12 May 1984:C1.

34 Paul Delean, "Montreal benefits Hong Kong investment," MG, reprinted in CN, 18 May 1985:8.

35 Janet Bagnall, "Chinatown Blues," MG, 15 March 1997:B1.

36 Richard I. Mann, Canada Our Land (Toronto: Gateway Books, 1986), 129.

37 Jerry Collins, "Immigrants find Montreal's lifestyle a relaxed pace," CN, 3 June 1991:7.

38 Bagnall, "Chinatown Blues."

39 Sidhartha Banerjee, "Chinatown: symbolic heart of the community," MG, 9 Feb. 2002:H9.

40 Linda Gyulai, "Italian, Greek being eclipsed by recent immigrants," MG, 11 Dec. 2002:A3.

41 Kenneth Cheung, "Sticking to its guns: Chinatown should take action," MG, 5 March 1998:B3.

42 Canadian Press Newswire, 25 Dec. 1997.

43 George Kalogerakis, "Standing up for Diversity: Chinatown defies sign crackdown," MG 5 Feb. 1998:A1.

44 Doug Sweet, "Heat's off Chinatown merchants – for now," MG, 23 June 1998:A3.

45 Alexander Noriss, "Immigrants see little profit in separation," MG, 17 Oct. 1995:D4.

HALIFAX

1 Acadian Recorder (hereafter AR) 20 Nov. 1890:3; 15 Jan. 1891:3; 2 April 1891.

2 AR, 13 June 1894:3

3 Larry Shyu, Chinese (Halifax: Nimbus Books, 1997), 20.

4 AR, 26 Sept. 1905:3; 28 Feb. 1911:3.

5 AR, 16 April 1912:3

6 AR, 19 May 1914:2.

7 AR, 23, 24 April 1906:3.

8 AR, 28 Sept. 1909: 3.

9 Huang Jin, International Chinese Business Directory, 1913, 1385.

10 Halifax Herald, (hereafter HH) 7 May 1918.

11 HH, 13 Feb. 1919.

12 HH, 19 Feb. 1919.

13 HH, 28 Feb. 1919.

14 CT, 5 Feb. 1918 in CCRC 4:7; 20 Feb. 1920 in CCRC 4:8; Judith Fingard, J. Guildford and D. Sutherland, Halifax: the First 250 Years (Halifax: Formac, 1999), 139.

15 The Maritime Merchant, 11 July 1918: 28.

16 HH, 28 Feb. 1919.

17 HH, 15 March 1919.

18 HH, 28 March 1919.

19 HH, 28 Aug. 1920.

20 HH, 28 Feb. 1919, 16 Oct. 1920.

21 HH, 2 May 1919.

22 HH, 17, 22 Dec. 1923.

23 HH, 1 April 1924

24 Michael Scott Boudreau, "Crime and Society in a City of Order: Halifax 1918-1935," Ph.D dissertation, Queen's University, 1996, 456–58.

25 Wickberg, China to Canada, 224.

26 HH, 15 June 1920.

27 Albert Lee, "Growing Up Chinese in Halifax," shunpiking (June 1999):11.

28 CT, 23 April 1929 in CCRC 4:19.

29 HH, 3 Jan., 27 March 1922.

30 HH, 16 June 1924.

31 CT, 25 July 1931 in CCRC 4:15.

32 Wickberg, China to Canada, 305.

33 CT, 14 Oct. 1938 in CCRC Box 5:3.

34 CT, 2 Nov. 1938 in CCRC Box 5:3.

35 Chai-Chu Thompson, "Chinese Community of the Halifax-Dartmouth Area," Your World, International Education Centre Newsletter (1981):23.

36 Public Archives of Nova Scotia, MG 100, Vol. 59 #2, 2. Chuck Lee interviewed by Lynn Murphy, 25 January 1984 (hereafter Lee interview).

37 Lee interview, 5.

38 Lee interview, 6.

39 Lee interview, 6.

40 CN, 18 Oct. 1971:41.

41 "Machine Replaces Laundryman." CN, 3 Sept, 1967:10.

42 Ann Quon, "A Church of Their Own," HH, 7 Dec. 2002.

43 David Redwood, "Dragon breathes fire into winter," Halifax Daily News (hereafter HDN) 6 Feb.2000:3.

44 Shyu, Chinese, 23.

45 David Swick, "New Asian foodmart adds to delicious Quinpool," HDN, 17 Feb. 1997:2 .

46 Bill Power, "Out of work, far from home," HH, 12 Feb. 2003.

47 Shyu, Chinese, 43.

48 Thompson, "Chinese Community," 22.

# PHOTO CREDITS

David Barbour, pp 1C, 90, 98

Stacey Curtis, p 23

Archives nationales du Quebec, P405 S11 P348, p103; Archives nationales du Quebec/Conrad Poirier, P48 S1 P5301, p104; P48 S1 P12331, p105

Archives of Ontario, RG14-151-3-157, p77; RG 47-42, p88; Archives of Ontario/John Boyd, C7-2 Box E341, C7-2-0-1-33, p78

British Columbia Archives, C-01274, p12; D-01660, p15; I-03395, p25; B-01653, p27; C-07939, p29T; E-02063, p29B; D-08821, p31; B-01010, p33; I-03391, p37; I-03368, p38; A-04437, p41; D-00335, p43T

British Columbia Archives/Canadian Illustrated News, 1879-04-26, James L. Weston, PDP 01873, p26; British Columbia Archives/Cecil Clarke, F-00351, p35; British Columbia Archives/Josephine Crease, PDP 02161, p30; British Columbia Archives/Hannah Maynard, A-04599, p28T

Bibliotheque Nationale de Quebec/Fonds Massicotte, 2-238-b, p100B; 3-168-a, p101

Calgary Chinese Cultural Centre, p 54

Calgary Chinese United Church, pp 59, 60T, 60B

Canadian Museum of Civilization, p69B; Canadian Museum of Civilization/P.C. Chan, 77-541, p106; Canadian Museum of Civilization/Catherine Collins, #996.9.1, p68

City of Vancouver Archives, Add. MSS 369 Box 552-D-5, p46

Glenbow Archives, NA 2798-6, p57T; NA 2799-2, p58; 5600-8207a, p 61; Glenbow Archives/Jean Andrews, PA 3546 file 15 #34, p63T; Glenbow Archives/Boorne and May, NA 387-27, p55; Glenbow Archives/Dawson, PA2807-2189(a), p18; Glenbow Archives/Frank Halliday, NA 5520-1, p57B; Glenbow Archives/Alison Jackson, NA 2645-48, p 62T; NA 2645-52, p62B; Glenbow Archives/Snider and Curlette, NA 2575-4, p56

William Joe, 92

A Selective Collection of Hong Kong Historic Postcards, Hong Kong: Joint Publishing Co., 1993, p 10T

Donald and Mabel Kwan, p96

Albert Lee, front cover BC, pp 1L, 11, 111, 112, 113, 116, 117, 118, 119

Keith Lock, 34, 79, 80, 83

La Presse, 1904-01-11, p100T

Library Archives of Canada, PA-118183, p28B; PA 124939, p82; Library Archives of Canada/Marik Boudreau, 1991-067#16, p21; 1991-067, Photo #7, p107; Library Archives of Canada/John Boyd, PA-87321, p81; Library Archives of Canada/Duncan Cameron, E002113674, p95; Library Archives of Canada/Suzanne Girard, 1991-067, Photo #21, p108T; 1991-067, Photo #19, p108B; Library Archives of Canada/Globe and Mail PA 124939, 1R; Library Archives of Canada/Chris Lund, PA 112803, p94; Library Archives of Canada/Edward Roper, 1989-176-37, p40; Library Archives of Canada/William Topley, E002505263, p91; PA 043135, p93

Lim, Sing, West Coast Chinese Boy, Tundra, 1979, pp 16, 44

Manitoba Chinese Historical Society, pp 10B, 14

Manitoba Museum, p69T

Mary Mohamed, front cover TR, BL, pp 114, 115

Manitoba Chinese Historical Society, pp 67, 70, 72T, 74

Office of Senator Poy, p97

University of British Columbia, Museum of Anthropology, p53

University of British Columbia, Special Collections, Chinese Canadian Research Collection, Box 10, file 13, p32; Wallace Chung Collection, FOLDR 0016, p45; Chung Collection A-6-1, p48; Chung Collection, p72B

University of Manitoba, Archives and Special Collections, PC18-1568-004, p71

Vincenzo Pietropaolo, pp 8, 22, 24 85, 86, 89

Vancouver Public Library/ N. H. Hawkins, 39046, p13; 39047, p43B

www.viewcalgary.com/Peter Reath, #0532, p64; #0621, p65

Paul Yee, pp 39, 47, 49, 51, 66, 75, 76, 99, 110, 63B, 84B, 84T, 36, 20

# INDEX